INFIDEL: KAFIR

INFIDEL: KAFIR

Bernard MacDonald

CITI OF
BOOKS

CITIOFBOOKS, INC.
3736 Eubank NE Suite A1
Albuquerque, NM 87111-3579
www.citiofbooks.com
Hotline: 1 (877) 389-2759
Fax: 1 (505) 930-7244

Ordering Information:

Quantity sales. Special discounts are available on quantity purchases by corporations, associations, and others. For details, contact the publisher at the address above.

Printed in the United States of America.

ISBN-13:   Softcover   979-8-89391-998-1
                  eBook   979-8-89391-999-8

Library of Congress Control Number: 2025925260

TABLE OF CONTENTS

ACKNOWLEDGMENT

Many thanks to Carolyn Rhodes who pushed me to improve and add important passages and edit, edit, edit! Thanks Marv & Salessa B. for encouragement as always, and thanks for a first reading by Carol S.

FOREWORD

Only Breath

Not Christian or Jew or Muslim, not Hindu Buddhist, sufi, or zen.

Not any religion or cultural system.

I am not from the East or the West, not out of the ocean or up from the ground, not natural or ethereal, not composed of elements at all.

I do not exist, am not an entity in this world or in the next, did not descend from Adam and Eve or any origin story.

My place is placeless, a trace of the traceless.

Neither body or soul.

I belong to the beloved, have seen the two worlds as one and that one call to and know, first, last, outer, inner, only that breath breathing human being. From Rumi

INFIDELKAFIR

Infidel: a person who does not believe in a religion or who adheres to a religion other than ones own.

CHAPTER ONE

6:45 AM, August 10, 2011

Daly City, California

Atiyah sits at her little black metal table, bright flowered table cloth, in her bright butter yellow kitchen alcove of her apt in the Daly City section of San Francisco. She watches the morning crowd go by on their way to grab a bus or the Bay Area Rapid Transit (BART) to work. She sips her coffee, which is dark and strong, so different from the strong tea of her youth in Iraq. She herself must be off in a few minutes, but now enjoys a second cup of coffee. Her thoughts drift to a day long ago, over 6 years now, walking through the bazaar in Jamilla, Iraq, with David close by, observing a far different crowd. Remembering the reaction of women, like herself covered in traditional abaya which is like a coat, and the hijab covering the head like a scarf and a niqab scarf covers her lower face.

"Look at them, the eyes, which Muslim women read so clearly. They have judged me as sinful to be with this Western man in public. Surely word will get back to Um Muammar, and he will sternly speak to me about this public display. But then, with David next to me, my

1

heart was warmed, the world seemed not so harsh, and my desire to know this man better was strong."

She displayed a stubborn streak even then, and defied tradition by being with this infidel in public. David was a marine then, helping villagers with reconstruction after the invasion of Baghdad. She had received a scholarship years ago, and studied nursing in the West. She had family connections in the states and they helped her find scholarship money to send her to school. It was no easy task under Saddam to acquire a student visa but she had persevered. After graduation, and working a couple of years, she reluctantly came back to Baghdad to help her elderly father.

She had learned the ways and culture of the Western mind and their mannerisms were not unknown to her, but it was far different to be with a Western man in her hometown of Jamilla, a small city outside Baghdad. But all that was in the past now. It seemed so long ago but the memories were still so strong.

She sees the clock on her kitchen wall, which brings her back to the here and now. Time to leave for work. She pushes her thoughts aside and giving a long sigh takes her cup to the sink and readies herself for work. As she glances in the mirror she notes the gray starting to show in her jet black hair, with natural curl, which is kept shoulder length, often pulled back. She has dark black eyes, high cheek bones, a slim nose, full lips and her figure is still slim. She is tall at 5' 8", a runner when time allows, and works out at the hospital gym at least 3 times a week. At 32 years old she values these opportunities to take care of herself more than most, knowing how poorly women are treated in many parts of the world. She sees her Kurdish roots reflected in the shop windows as she hurries to the station. Admires her bright yellow blouse and black skirt with a colorful scarf around her neck, she notes with a smile that this would not be acceptable in Jamilla, there the women surely would talk quietly amongst themselves with catty mewings of envy.

On the Bay Area Rapid Transit BART), with so many other riders packed in like sardines she is headed into the city to her job as an intensive care nurse with University of California, San Francisco hospital. She has time to think back to her father, Muammar, as everyone called him, because he was a respected patriarch in the community. He had been a constant force in her upbringing from a young age when her mother had been killed and her father had been seriously injured in reprisals from the Baath party under Saddam. He had worked hard, even with his disabilities, to build up the leather goods shop located next to the small home where they lived. At his advanced age, her father was often furious at the United States for invading his country. His original homeland was Kurdistan to the north of Baghdad. Most of his family lived in Kurdistan and they had been happy to see the U.S. invasion since they believed this would lead to an independent Kurdish homeland.

Saddam Hussein ruled Iraq from 1958 until 2003 when the U.S., under President George Bush, invaded Iraq, in the campaign known as "Shock and Awe". This invasion was based on a belief that Saddam was building and hiding *weapons of mass destruction."* But when U.S. troops invaded, and tried to find these weapons, there were none to find. Bush made the case that Saddam was not to be trusted and was a tyrant. The problem with that argument is that the world is filled with tyrants. Which ones do we pick to overthrow? At what cost? The U.S. Marines hunted Saddam down and turned him over to the new Iraqi government put in place by the U.S.. The initial "shock" was the use of thousands of 500 pound bombs and cruise missiles that did destroy many military targets but also destroyed many homes and businesses of innocent civilians and killed thousands of innocent civilians as well. Let alone over 4,000 young men and women of the coalition forces were killed in the subsequent fighting.

There was not much "awe"! More like "ah shucks"! As Iraq quickly spiraled out of control and sectarian violence threatened to tear the country apart. In the last few years, 2006-2011, as U.S. forces and coalition forces were drawn down, violence has subsided, but sectarian hatred and subsequent violence continues, though at a much reduced level.

Atiyah's father Muamar, was devastated and angered when the bombs began to fall. He realized not only was his family in Jamilla in danger, but his leather goods business was in danger of being crushed. Months went by and the bombs seemed not to be aimed at their little part of the Muslim world, but one early May morning, about three AM, the world blew up, literally, in their faces. The walls caved in, the noise was thunderous, and the air was sucked out of their little house which was located next to the shop. Within seconds the air came back ten times worse with debris and dust choking them as they fled for their lives. Surprisingly, they realized they were alive! Bruised, scratched, and temporarily deafened but alive! They didn't know which way to go or what to do to protect themselves.

The dust settled and it was clear they had no home to stay in or a business to go back to. They could hear the scream of women close by and men were yelling and trying to find those buried in rubble. All was a pile of stone, dirt, concrete, and now flames and smoke rose from the remnants of houses and buildings here and there. They grabbed whatever they could and tried to smother the flames but little could be salvaged.

After checking on neighbors and realizing they were in shock they squatted in the few bare patches of earth and cried and yelled until finally they had had enough and knew they needed to find some place to stay. They asked up and down the streets and finally found neighbors whose house still stood. For a Muslim not to take in a neighbor in need would be unthinkable. The Qur'an or more common in English, *Koran*, speaks to this when Mohammed states, *"Help ye one another in righteousness and piety."*

They were invited to stay with these neighbors a few blocks away. Their house had been spared from the destruction but had they had nothing but a few rooms and a courtyard where they cooked. The courtyard was dried dirt with some old tiles placed here and there and a few metal chairs and one wooden bench. A few sad looking plants in pots looked as beaten as the people sharing this space. One medium sized lemon tree grew against a back wall, as well as an old grape vine. Cooking was done on an old metal stove with a little door so wood could be thrown in, lighted, and given some time produce a decent fire for cooking. The two families were stuffed together with only a carpet and pillows for a bed and stayed in the courtyard most of the day. They had water only a few hours a day if that, and had to fill jugs, pots, anything to store water for cooking. Washing and bathing were not possible unless they had a good couple of days and the electricity stayed on longer than usual. Even the sewers were backing up and the streets in places smelled of sewage. This was not what Atiyah had imagined when she decided to come back here but what could be done now? She could not leave her father, he was not well and her bother Siamak was not around much and usually in a foul mood when he was home. The line of refugees at the borders was miles long and she knew her father would not survive such a trek.

They stayed and prayed for conditions to improve and little by little they had. When a neighbor told them about the offer from the U.S. marines to rebuild the house and shop, Atiyah had taken her father to the Green Zone and applied for assistance. He was a proud man and not happy to be shuffling in front of these intruders, these infidels, but what could he do? He needed help. He could not keep his family living in this wretched way, sleeping in the open most nights and huddling in small dirt floored rooms when it rained or was too cold.

Atiyah also recalled how the U.S. invasion had changed their lives. Not for the better as the U.S. leadership promised, but mostly for the worse. Before the invasion, Saddam kept harsh, sometimes brutal control over the various sectarian groups but no one dared to go after a rival group for fear of the reprisal from Saddam's forces and the police who would crush any uprising. There was peace and security even if little freedom. After the invasion her neighbors started to fight over old family grudges between Shia and Sunni tribes. The Shia were driven out and only Sunni's and some Kurd's such as her family remained in her neighborhood. Each faction saw a political advantage in driving the other out of Iraq.

CHAPTER TWO

7:10 AM, August 10, 2011

Daly City, California

Back in Daly City, Atiyah looked out the window of the train as it came out of the tunnel to her station, and whispered to herself, "If Allah wills it.." "Enshallah". She grabbed her things and headed up the station stairs to the sunshine and bustle of the city. She had only a few blocks to walk and it was a pleasant walk most mornings. The air was cool on her face but the early morning sun slanting between the glass and stone of these tall city buildings brought some warmth.

"I wonder if he's alive and well? Where could he be if he is alive? Not with his parents I'm sure, and I can't believe back in Iraq, so where? Or he's dead and I'll never know.

She thinks back to how they had met. She had brought her father, Muamar, to see the young officer Captain David Goldman, to apply for a grant to repair his leather goods shop which was destroyed in the bombing. Her father at first was against having any contact with these infidels, these "invaders" as he called them. Especially when introduced to this Jew soldier, David Goldman! He must have also

7

resented his daughters education which had taken her to the States for 5 years and away from her home. He had been proud when she showed him her degree in nursing and when she decided to come home to help him as his health was failing but now this same country had invaded and their bombs destroyed his little business he worked so hard to build."

She had Googled his name, David Goldman, and got nothing that was recent. His college degrees, enlistment and promotion to captain were there, but nothing in the last year. She didn't really expect to find anything recent knowing he would be protecting his identity. If he had been captured by extremist he would be missing for years before any evidence became public unless they used him for the "cause" and had behead him in a video to put the fear of Allah in the minds of anyone working with U.S. or coalition forces. She found nothing to support this scenario so believed he was alive somewhere. But where?

As plans had moved ahead fixing her father's shop and living quarters Atiyah had assumed more control over the business and this required more and more meetings with the American soldiers and civilians who administered the funding. She attended many meetings both inside and outside the Green Zone. She remembered the first time she was alone with David. He was curious about how she had been schooled in the states and after a degree in nursing returned here to this little place with her father. They were in the new addition to the shop going over the blueprints and some changes Atiyah wanted to make. She was next to him, his aftershave pleasant to her senses, wondering if he noticed her also? She was dressed in a dark blue kurti or dress with tight black pants under and a light blue scarf around her head. She untied her scarf and started to tie it back when David turned to her and with direct eye contact said, "Don't! Your hair is too pretty to be covered! Sorry, not my place..... but wow! You are a pretty women and I couldn't help myself!"

She found herself blushing but inwardly pleased to be noticed by him. She put the scarf around her shoulders and returned his look and could feel the magnetism between them, she knew if she leaned in any closer they would kiss. She told herself, "No! You can not! Not here! Not now!"

But even as she said it he leaned in and lightly, lightly as the wings of a butterfly kissed her lips. She responded just as lightly but pulled back looking deeply into his dark eyes.

"This can not be David. Surely you know that? I must go tend to my father. Please excuse me." With a shy bow she turned and left the room.

When they met again he had apologized and had let her know he would not do that again. However, as is often the case with the best of intentions they spent more and more time with each other, at the remodeled house, business and in the bazaar where they would linger over blueprints and talk for hours.

Soon enough she was thinking and plotting how they could meet? Where could they go to have more freedom from prying eyes. The answer came, from of all places, her father! He had been turning over more of the business to her and had requested she go to Istanbul to purchase supplies for the shop.

One morning as they had been talking in the shop she mentioned to David, "I will be gone for a few days next week. I must go to Istanbul to buy supplies for my father."

David looked a little hurt and responded, "Oh, I love Istanbul! Lucky you! I'll miss you though, and I think you know that? Yes?"

"No, no, you will be busy with so many people who need your help."

"I have leave coming, I could take some time off. Would you be interested in me meeting you there? No, not in the same place. I would get my own room. But we could have a good time seeing the city and walking the bazaar."

"Oh, that would be nice but I, I don't know.... if my father ever heard of this..... let me think about it, OK?"

Next day she told him, "Yes, if you are sure? I would love to see you in Istanbul but as friends, yes? Let's make some plans for that OK?"

And as they say, the rest was history! They had wonderful walks, and he thought back to the second day he was there with her and she asked him back to her room. He was very hesitant but went with a bottle of wine in hand. They sat at the little table by the window in her room drinking wine, nibbling on a plate of Turkish olives, cheese and crusty bread and then nibbling on each other. Damn, it was nice! She finally led him to her bed and they pulled at each others clothes and devoured each other in passion. They lay twisted around each other for hours until finally falling asleep.

Arriving at the hospital and the women's locker room, she quickly changed to her nurses scrubs and replaced her street shoes with the white work shoes she bought to give her feet support for the long hours walking on concrete floors.

"Hi Atty!!" caused her to look up and see her fellow nurse and friend Barb coming in to change.

"Hi Barb, how's the family? Is Billy over the flu?"

"Not quite but he's doing much better. His temp is down and he's eating a little. At least John and I got some sleep! God we needed it!"

"Gotta run and get something to eat in the cafeteria. Want to join me?"

"Yeah, sure, give me a minute. I'll see you down there!"

Sitting with a yogurt and coffee Barb looked across the table in the cafeteria of the hospital, a modern light filled space with large windows that looked out on green spaces and plantings of trees and flowering bushes, and inquired, "Atty, what's with you lately? You seem absorbed in something? What's up?"

"Oh, I don't know Barb, it's not always easy to forget the past and how I ended up here. I mean, I love working here and having good friends like you but lately my mind keeps wandering back to what happened in Baghdad. I just can't let go of a feeling that it's not resolved. What if David wasn't killed? I wonder if he's still somewhere around Baghdad looking for me. Crazy I know. I have no family now and yet life is good, why can't I just go on?"

"Jeez Louis! I don't know anybody that's gone through what you went through and I'm sure nobody would blame you for doubts and for wanting closure. Do you think you should go back for more counseling?"

"No, I'm finished with counseling. It's OK, thanks for listening. Let's get going, we're due on the floor." sighs Atiyah with resignation.

What she thought, but didn't say was how hard it was to just "*get on with it*"! She thought of him almost every day. There was no resolution. Was he alive? Was he dead? Did he think of her? The feeling was like a rock she carried, in her heart, if she had to name a place. The rock was smaller now, rounded and smooth from time, but it was there and she supposed it would eventually be nothing but a grain of sand, lost in the desert of memories she carries from her past.

She and Barb took the elevator to the 5th floor, signed in and reported to their duty stations.

Atiyah was always curious and impressed with the different nationalities that she worked with on the ward. Name a nationality and she swears she has worked with them. Even her own Kurdish people have been her patients. Just two months ago she worked with an old Kurdish gentleman, 80 + years and cantankerous as he could be, but she grew to enjoy him. He was impressed when she spoke their native Kurdish language, not just Arabic to him. He grew to respect her and they shared many lovely memories. He was there for heart surgery and sadly did not make it through the surgery. This man reminded her of her elderly father who was struck down by a stroke and died shortly after they had come to the states. She felt sure her father died as much from loneliness as anything else. Atiyah had learned to live with and accept these lost lives in her job. She often saw patients who were in the last chapter of life or for some, last pages. She was OK with this since she also knew they often had a long and interesting life. She had experienced losing so many healthy, robust men and women in Baghdad, torn apart by bombs and bullets. The hardest part for her in her nursing job, was the young children who came in with illness or serious injuries from an accident and it was clear they would not make it. She would steel herself for the sadness that would come all too soon.

CHAPTER THREE

1:45 PM, September 12, 2011

Baghdad, Iraq

After undergoing a search at the entry checkpoint, David Goldman 45 years old, pushes through the bazaar, an outdoor market in Baghdad, filled with fresh vegetables, spices, meats, cheese and flat breads, as well as small cafes where you would find men sitting at tables smoking flavored Turkish tobacco through a hooka and sipping strong black tea, called chai, with tons of sugar. The aisles are jammed with people, mostly men dressed in black, brown and white, as he is. He is assailed by strange, yet pleasant smells from tables piled high with herbs, spices, and strange fruits he knows the name of only a few. There are stalls with leather goods, clothing, brass utensils, silver, jewelry, kitchen items, and foods of all kinds. His eyes always watchful for her face, her eyes, even though he has resigned himself to the loss, his heart will not completely let go. It has been years and he is lucky to be alive.

Given what took place years ago now, his buddies can't believe that he would ever want to be in this city again, but he is not so unusual when it comes to wanting to be back in a place where you feared for your life. He has many buddies from his time in the military here who have signed up for repeated tours of duty. Something about the danger and the belief that you are making a real difference in peoples lives brings soldiers back time and again. He faces less danger now with his job, mostly driving around from one clinic to another but also there are those crazy Taliban types who don't want any help from outsiders, especially infidels. He of course has the additional burden placed on his shoulders from previously being kidnapped here in Baghdad. He uses an alias in his work. He is *Daniel White* to his colleagues and the people he works with out in the neighborhoods. He is assigned to the staff of Doctors Without Borders (DWB) to organize and staff new clinics in Baghdad.

Often in his free time he goes back to the neighborhood of Jamilla where Atiyah's family was from, and wanders the streets, now lined with concrete blast walls, looking for what, he does not really know. His Arabic is quite passable now and he doesn't stand out as much in the crowds. He is dark complected, dark brown eyes, salt and pepper hair, let go to shoulder length, and sporting a trimmed beard. He does have a strong Roman nose and high cheek bones but that also is not uncommon in this part of the world. He wears Western clothes but muted colors and styled so as not to attract undue attention.

His position with Doctors Without Borders allows him a fair amount of free time and his military pension is enough that he has an apartment in one of the better parts of the city. There are blast walls erected around his neighborhood, as in many parts of the city. Few people walk around at night, but unlike when he first came to this part of the world, the constant threat of violence is far less, but always lurking outside your neighborhood. Electricity is still limited to 3 or 4 hours in the afternoon and evening but his neighborhood pays a private contractor to provide power the rest of the day.

What is he looking for as he roams these streets? All that happened in the past is exactly that, past! Why brood over it? After all the trouble, his kidnapping, the transfer stateside, something inside has stayed unsettled.

He did go back to the states for awhile, and he tried to fit in but he couldn't get her out of his head and heart. He also missed trying to help the common people in Iraq, who had suffered much from the invasion. He and Atiyah had shared so much. Each had a religion based on the Middle East. Steeped in the mysteries of this ancient place, each had been raised with prejudice toward the other, at least the other as defined by family and religious leaders. She had grown up knowing that Jew were the infidel and were the enemy of Islam. He had grown up hearing the angry words used toward muslims and Israel was the jewish homeland. It must be protected at all costs against the Arab muslims. His family lived in Philadelphia, not in Israel, but there was still plenty of talk about Israel and the wars against the Arabs.

David had survived the kidnapping, most of the bad guys were dead, and he was left with some bad scars where his captors cut him when the Special Ops guys had stormed in, but most of the damage may have been mental. He still has nightmares bringing him back in that hot, fetid space, his eyes covered with a rag, another pulled across his mouth, his hands and legs bound, the feel of a dirt floor under him, stone walls against his back.

He can still hear them talking fast and scared as they had been warned the Americans are getting close. The one who had been his "keeper" bent close to him, he can still smell his breath, mint from his tea.

He hears whispers through clenched teeth, "If infidels get here you die my friend! Enshallah!" He can hear him, smell him as if it was yesterday. Then everything was a blur! Crack! Whump! The air was instantly hot, pushed out of his lungs. Bright light explodes, even with his eyes covered he had seen the flash of light and instantly chemical smells assailed his nostrils. He was knocked unconscious as were his captors. He woke being carried outside by a marine and rushed into a Humvee, given some kind of medicine to clear his mind.

Later he found the Spec Ops guys had used a stun grenade to knock out everyone in the room and allow safe entry for a rescue.

CHAPTER FOUR

3:45 AM, September 13, 2011

Baghdad, Iraq

He wakes now from his nightmare, early morning, in his room, sweating even with the AC on. He feels his throat where the scars ripple under his fingers. He lets his mind wander back to when he was released days after, from the hospital in the Green Zone. When he had returned to Jamilla and Atiyah's families house and found nobody. The family house and shop next door, had been with David's help, partially repaired after the bombings and the family allowed to move back in until the rest could be renovated.

After his kidnapping he later found that Atiyah was to be included in the kidnapping because of her involvement with David. In the end they had left her out and instead settled for the American Jew. He had gone back to find the Rashid's house vacant, no sign of the old man, no sign of Atiyah. He had gone in, sat on the couch and stared at the walls wondering what had happened? He could still smell her here, amongst the debris that still littered most of the rooms. He had found on the floor, in a corner, a Turkish ring she would caress when he had been with her.

His memory of the scene now was as if they had just vanished into thin air. He had gone to neighbors and asked of them, only to be met with, "Al- salamu' Alaikum! They gone, we know nothing! Not here. You go, no trouble!"

When pressed for a date when the kidnapping took place and for how long he was abducted, the best he could do was some number of days from the time he had been rescued from his captors. He still had no clear recollection of the time span.

When he had been released from the hospital, he went back to his headquarters in the Green Zone, and asked what had happened to the Rashid family? Since he was the officer who had been working with them to repair their house and business he thought he had a right to know if they were safe. His commanding officer had called him in and gave him a debriefing, along with the commander James Bryson, of the Spec Ops team that had freed him.

He can clearly remember the scene in Colonel Bryson's office,

"David, you had no idea that this family had contacts with an Al Qaeda cell? We had Siamak's name and some intel that he was in a cell and they were actively looking for a target. You and Atiyah Rashid apparently came up on their radar."

A puzzled David responded, "No idea, not a clue!"

"Did you know the brother of Atiyah Rhashid? Siamak?"

"Atiyah had mentioned him but I had no direct info that he was in any way connected to Al Qaeda! I never met the man."

David's commander, Joe Heffington with a look of disbelief had then spoken up. "Look Captain, I'm not going to mince words here. There is some indication you and this woman, Atiyah, had a relationship that was not appropriate. Can you deny that or want to tell us more?

David jumped back with anger in his voice, "I think at this time I will not dignify that comment and I can't see how that would lead to what happened?"

Joe, face red with anger, jumped on this! "You don't!! For Christ sake man! She is Muslim, her brother had connections to an Al Qaeda cell and you can't see any reason you might end up being kidnapped by that same cell! Oh man, I'm so close to court marshaling your ass!"

Just as an angry David shot back with, "What the fuck is this a set up? Do I need legal counsel?"

"David, I can't answer that but I'll tell you what I'm going to do!"

And in no uncertain words, he had told him he was finished with his assignment and would be reassigned stateside within 30 days. He was ordered not to inquire about any of his families, especially the Rashid family.

He had sputtered, "But sir......" and was quickly rebuffed, "Captain, this conversation is finished! You are finished here, do you understand my orders?"

"Yes, sir. Am I excused?"

"You are! Good day!" Shouted Heffington, his face red with anger.

He had stood, saluted them both, and thanked James Bryson for his rescue.

He was seething when he came out of the office and gone back to his barracks. He had been told to take leave immediately and standby on base for orders.

He had later learned the Marine Spec Ops team had contacts feeding intel on Siamak and his cell. The team knew only hours before the kidnapping what was going down but they had no idea where or exactly when. They had lost contact once he was abducted and only a stroke of luck when a marine patrol had brought up some intel chatter and following up on this found the abandoned house where he was being held.

He knew he had been lucky and he also recognized his commander had been right to be pissed. He had violated so many rules by letting this woman into his life and crossing boundaries that led to this terrible event. It's one thing to put his life in harms way but he had also involved the men in the Spec Ops unit and changed Atiyah's life forever and also her dear father whom he had come to like and respect.

Atiyah's brother Siamak was tried for kidnapping, assault, and terrorism with intent to kill and sent to prison. David learned he spent only 3 years in prison before he and many others escaped from the poorly guarded prison. The fact that Siamak was on the loose did not make David's life any easier but he felt his new identity gave him some feeling of safety.

When he did return from his leave he found his desk cleared and all his files on families he had been working with were gone. When he inquired what happened to his files, his superior, Colonel Bryson, a fireplug with requisite salt and pepper military flat top hair, told him they were not his concern any longer. He was, at this point to stay at his desk and he would not be going out in the community without direct orders to do so. He was reassigned to routine paperwork and a week later had received orders reassigning him stateside to Blacksburg, Virginia.

He finished out his 20 years with the service 2 years ago and retired not knowing what he was going to do with himself. His mother and father wanted him to return to Philly but he just couldn't do it. He did go to visit for a couple of weeks but he needed something else to make him feel whole again. He was no longer the "good jewish boy" his mother would praise so often it made his head hurt! He had completed college, joined the service, completed Officer Candidate School, had postings at a number of bases stateside and in Saudi Arabia where he studied Arab culture and language, then found himself sent to Iraq helping with rebuilding a city that was badly damaged and not functioning.

He found himself immersed in a culture that was so foreign and yet on some level so familiar. So many of the places from the bible were located here or close to here. City names he had read so many times in the Old Testament. This was the land of Mesopotamia, with the Tower of Babel located along with Babylonia just south of Baghdad. Here also lies the famous ziggurat and Aqar Ouf, the largest and oldest brick formed arch still standing. The city was famous because of it's geography, lying between the Tigris and Euphrates rivers. Babylon had been located here as well as the biblical city of Ur which is known as the biblical home of Abraham, Daniel and David. He had

Working in Baghdad with families in need had been the best job he had encountered in his military or civilian life. Now he felt lucky to have found this position with Doctors Without Borders (DWB) and it also gave him a feeling of accomplishment. He was not on the front lines but his work allowed for the medical care of many people who had no access to care otherwise. He was employed to coordinate the building, supplying and running of medical clinics in the Baghdad region. Since DWB often worked in sensitive areas of the world they provided complete anonymity to their workers and this he appreciated. He did not want anyone from the extremist groups here in Baghdad to recognize his name on the internet and come looking for him to finish what they had started. When he was in the states he had made several attempts to find Atiyah. Surfing the internet he found her record of graduation from nursing school at the University of Maryland, but nothing recently. Of course he realized if she was still in Jamilla, a suburb of Baghdad he would not find anything on the internet. The use of the internet was growing rapidly but there just was not the infrastructure needed to bring the common man in the street into a data engine search. He had pretty much resigned himself to not knowing where she was, except for the occasional drive through her neighborhood.

CHAPTER FIVE

9:00 AM, Wednesday June 14, 2005

Baghdad, Iraq

Siamak is sitting in the bazaar, dressed in camo trousers and scruffy white T-shirt, feeling the coolness of the morning on his shoulders, knowing it will be hot by 12 noon. His longish black curly hair looks unwashed, his dark black eyes scan the crowds for trouble. Others are looking for him since his escape from the Iraqi prison. He is having tea, sucking on a hooka pipe, rethinking all that has happened and feeling the burn of anger for his sister and especially for that infidel Jew she was accompanying around the neighborhood! She even had the nerve to disrespect their father and walk him into the Green Zone which is filled with infidels!

His thoughts go back to when he began to feel a yearning as a young man, about 18, for something more in his life. His close friend Abida was the one who talked to him of jihad and how he could find peace and a purpose in life. At first he couldn't see it, he had a father with a business that he could inherit some day, he had a decent life, why screw it up? But little by little he listened to Abida and saw how he changed. He stopped smoking, he stopped cursing and he talked of how Allah had a higher calling for him for which he would be rewarded in the next life. Abida had become physically strong and also strong and resolved in his mind; while Siamak just hung around smoking, helping his father in his shop and lusting after women walking by, their pretty dark eyes downcast.

Abida gave him a scolding look if he tried to share his thoughts. At first Siamak was annoyed but with reflection he began to admire his friend Abida. One day Abida was very serious and his face was a mask. He spoke of jihad against the foreigners, especially the Americans. The invasion had left many homeless and struggling and now his own father had lost his shop to a bomb. Day by day, Abida pointed out how arrogant the foreigners were. They dared to come into their country, tell them what was right and who must go! They took out Saddam without thinking about what might happen once they did this. Siamak was Kurdish but his friend Abida was Sunni and under Saddam this religious sect, even though a minority in population, controlled most of the civil organizations in Iraq. Now control was up for grabs and besides hating the Americans, Abida now vented his hatred for the other religious sect, the Shi'a who were gaining a voice in Iraqi government.

Siamak did see how arrogant the U.S. soldiers were and how disrespectful they were towards Muslim women. It made him feel ashamed to stand by and watch his country being taken by infidels and how his countrymen walked with heads down, accepting this humiliation. He saw more of his neighbors going to the mosque and he also started to attend, listening to the mullahs lecture on Muslim pride and history.

"We are a proud people, we were a great nation, the Persians were feared all across the regions of Mesopotamia. Now are we to kneel to these infidels who corrupt us each and every day? Are we to allow our women to mingle with these infidels? Our children corrupted by the taking of candy from these invaders walking our streets??"

This was the message he heard each week and it was making him angry. He needed to do something against these soldiers parading around in their Humvee's. He knew of others who were not sitting still but had joined with insurgent Al Qaeda to make improvised explosives. Abida told him he could join a cell with him and he would learn how to make weapons and how to place them so they would blow up the soldiers vehicles and they could shoot and kill the infidels when they ran. At first he went to these meetings, which were held in secret, not to kill but to learn how to stop the soldiers. He hoped they would decide it was not worth it and go home. But again, little by little it grew to an anger that would not be squelched.

Abida fed that anger and he made his first IED with Abida last year, designed to blow up and stop a tank. He had watched from a building across the street as the Humvee and convoy vehicles drove over the IED and it exploded blowing the Humvee over and stopping the convoy vehicles. Other Al Qaeda members watched from roof tops as the soldiers exited their vehicles dnucking for cover. Quite a few were shot as they tried to leave their vehicles and find cover. It bothered him at first, to see the soldiers shot, falling like sacks of grain or crawling like worms across the street and screaming in pain. He pushed that feeling down knowing many of his countrymen had suffered worse. It seemed fair to him, eye for an eye, tooth for a tooth.

Now he met Abida to ask his help in kidnapping his sister and perhaps the American Jew. He had seen them together with his father Um Muamar and also walking in the bazaar. Atiyah knew this was wrong and if she thought this was now permissible because of the Americans and the new regime she was sadly mistaken. She had gone to the states for her education and obviously now believed being with an infidel in public was permitted.

"As-Salaam Alaikum Abida, sit and we shall have tea."

"Walaikum As-Salaam my brother, and you are also well?" as he bows, hands folded in prayer, to Siamak.

Siamak returns a half bow, hands also folded, from his chair. "Yes and with Allah's blessing we shall prepare for our mission. I owe much to you Abida for bringing me the strength to know what is right and the courage to do so."

"I work only through Allah. Please, do we know where and when we could pick your sister up? and this infidel Jew?"

"Yes, I have watched her go each Tuesday and Thursday to the local bazaar for groceries. The Jew will not be as easy. I do not yet see a pattern to his visits but he is often at the shop in the morning."

"Siamak, we have eyes to watch and report when the Jew is there. This is not a problem. Now we must set a date and time and you must alert our comrades in the north so they may be there at the house where we will meet and bring honor back to you and your family."

Siamak and their brothers from the cell, took turns watching both Atiyah and David come and go at Muamars shop and made note of their routines. A pattern emerged with David coming most mornings to visit Siamak's father to help with rebuilding of his shop.

Siamak was now convinced in his desire to kidnap and execute the Jew but his heart had softened and he could not bring himself to do the same to his sister. He talked to Abida and asked that for now his sister be spared. His reasoning was that without David around his sister would find her true Muslim roots. Abida was in agreement that David, the Jew was a more important target for them and for Al Qaeda. They believed the Jew would bring them honor and prestige with the Al Qaeda leadership.

CHAPTER SIX

9:15 AM, Tuesday, July 12, 2005

Baghdad, Iraq

They knew David's routines well after watching him for days leaving the Green Zone and one hot July day they set out to execute their plan. They had enlisted one other cell mate to help with the capture and hiding of the Jew. They had the necessary phones, safe house and a car with stolen plates.

Siamak drove the car, and Abida and their comrade Tariq were ready to grab David when he came out of the Green zone, and headed toward Muamar's former shop, now in the beginning stages of being reconstructed.

As was always the case, the car was old, dirty but reliable, so no one would notice them sitting on the street.

"Look! Look! He just came out!" shouted Siamak!

Sure enough they observed David in his Humvee with another soldier driving, and David in the passenger seat, coming out through the Green zone checkpoint. They followed at a safe distance, knowing his route. Siamak stopped every half block or so and watched the Humvee making sure they were headed to Muamar's shop. They knew that the other soldier would take the Humvee back to the Green Zone and David would exit and walk into the shop alone. They counted on having enough time to grab him after the Humvee left before he entered the construction site. Now, they moved up closer to the Humvee, waited for the driver to pull up outside the shop. David got out, made small talk with the driver of his Humvee and turned to go into the shop.

The Humvee pulled away and Siamak yelled out the window as he pointed towards the Rashid shop, "Excuse soldier! Shop! Muamar Rashid?"

David stopped turned and walked a couple of steps towards the car.

In Arabic he said, "Yes, it was, do you need to see him? He may be inside."

"Yes, but also looking for daughter. You know? She here?"

This got David's attention and he moved closer. As he did Siamak, quickly checked his rearview mirror and said, quietly, "Tai-yip! (Now!)"

Tariq and Abida jumped out with pistols held down at their side, quickly moved up into David's face and said in broken accented English, "Do not theenk abut runneeng,yelling, you dead heeer!!"

They put the gun up to David's head. Tariq opened the back door and Abida pushed David into the back seat still holding the gun to David's head. Tariq ran to the other side and with David between them they pulled out plastic ties and bound his hands and feet even as David attempted to kick free. Using duct tape they covered his mouth and eyes. David had only brief glances of scraggy dark hair and long beards.

Siamak sped away to the safe house that was miles from the shop and Green Zone. They stayed away from busy streets. David had no chance to yell out for help and even if he was able to yell in Arabic no one would likely take notice since so much violence took place in these streets. They pulled up to the safe house in a screeching of brakes and clouds of dust. The nondescript house was in a run down part of town. There were old beat up cars, houses boarded up and looking as if they had not been lived in for a long time, bullet holes dancing across many of the brown mud walls. The safe house looked much the same with windows covered with plywood or dark curtains and security bars over the windows. They pulled up, looked around, saw no one and quickly dragged David, attempting to yell but to no avail, like a rolled up carpet, out of the car and into the house. They closed the door, turned on a feeble ceiling light and with David lying on the floor looking scared to death, went from room to room making sure all was clear. Coming back into the main room, they dragged David by his feet into a room in the back of the dimly lit house and left him there struggling against his bindings.

Abida was in touch with Faaris a fellow cell brother in Kurdistan who gave orders to wait for word when a comrade with video equipment would be there. They would be given instructions on making the video, speeches and with persuasion of torture make the infidel speak his lines begging U.S. forces to leave Iraq and also begging for his life.

Days went by and even Siamak was getting concerned. The house had no AC and no air since all the windows were boarded up or covered with dark drapes. Siamak would be left for hours guarding the Jew. He had enough food, though only food that was dried, or bread or fruit. He had bottled water and occasionally he gave some food and water to the Jew since he needed to keep him alive if they were to use him for a propaganda video. He was often bored but convinced himself Allah was testing his resolve and so he persevered, sweating, dozing, reading the Qur'an.

One early morning when he was sitting alone, guarding the Jew, bored and dozing once in awhile, suddenly the house blew up. One second he was dozing on a chair against the wall and the next his head seemed to explode! His eyes were blinded by a huge flash of light and all went black until he regained consciousness, finding himself handcuffed and trussed up in a Humvee with U.S. Marines surrounding him. He later learned the soldiers had found the safe house, busted down the door and thrown a stun grenade inside, knocking him and the Jew unconscious.

It was only a matter of weeks before he was turned over by U.S. soldiers to the new Iraqi police, sentenced by a judge to 20 years for kidnapping and assault and placed in an Iraqi prison. Conditions, were of course awful but the good news was escape was in the cards since most of the newly formed police recruits were corrupt. Some loyal Iraqi's paid for the guard's to look the other way and he and 5 or 6 others bolted from their cells one night. He worked his way back to Kurdistan to hide and wait for revenge.

CHAPTER SEVEN

2:30 AM, September 15, 2011

Baghdad, Iraq

David awoke, confused as to where he was, but then as he calmed himself, he knew it was his bedroom in Baghdad. He looked out the window. He could see the gold dome of the mosque lit against the night sky off in the distance. He was in Baghdad, in the middle of the night, sweat pouring down his face and chest, even with the AC blasting away. He knew, the dreams, flashbacks, whatever the doctors called them, were like living the events over and over. The kidnapping was years ago but still as he felt his arms, the wrists where he had been tied, it was as if they were bound even now. He remembered how his forehead hurt where the rags had been tight against his scalp for days on end. He had seen his captors for only seconds as they grabbed him by surprise. They had taken him as he got out of the Humvee to enter the Rashid house where he had been helping Muamar rebuild. As he was getting out of the vehicle and the driver had just left, they called to him from a car. He had walked over to talk to the man leaning out the window, when the man in the back seat and the man in the front seat jumped out holding guns to his head. They punched him in the stomach, knocking the air out of him, threw him in the back of the car, tied his hands and feet together behind his back, wrapped his head with duct tape cutting his mouth and blinding his eyes. He had never heard a name, short bursts of Arabic but nothing that would identify any of them, he lost track of time, days for sure, but how many he only found out on after his escape. He was usually held by at least two captors, but sometimes only one man who would talk to himself and mumble as he read the Qur'an. He could sometimes hear them speak in Arabic but little was revealed. They were well trained and knew not to speak in his presence any more than was necessary. A couple of times he heard a voice talk about him, "Dirty pig Jew! If I find you have been screwing one of our women infidel, I'll kill her too! She will have brought shame on her family." The other man in the room said, "Save your vengeance brother! He will be finished soon enough!" Sometimes they had told him he would be making a video and they threatened him with beheading but it never happened. He was left in darkness, time standing still and only his thoughts of escape which seemed hopeless unless his captors made a mistake. He was left with only breaks to relieve himself in a bottle, and eat, which consisted of rice, some meat, usually chicken, sometimes fish but never enough and seldom any vegetables. He could only tell time had passed when his captors came and went. The isolation was terrible, no light, no sense of day or night. After interminable darkness, lack of fresh air and daily threats he began to wish for it to be over. Death would be a release from this awful sensory deprivation with no hope in sight.

Now he woke laying in bed, calming himself and asking himself why he stayed here, back in the place where he had been kidnapped and tortured? He knew the dreams, the flashbacks would not stop just because he lived elsewhere but here he was still in a hostile land and as an American he was not always welcomed and if they knew he was a Jew many would be willing to turn him over to Al-Qaeda. He had lots of time to think while held in captivity back then. It was easy to hate the Muslims and many times he did but he also knew there were plenty of ultra religious Jews who hated Muslims and would kill them on sight if they came around their housing unit in the Golan Heights, or elsewhere on the West Bank. He knew of the hatred between Northern Ireland and the British, Catholic and Protestant, both Christian. How men who believed in the same God could do these horrible things in his name was no surprise to David. He hated these men for doing this to him but he could not hate Muslims as a whole. He had come to love and respect the people he worked with here in Baghdad and in fact had come to love a woman who was of their faith even if she no longer practiced the faith.

It all came down to a woman, didn't it? He missed her with all his heart. They had defied every convention, found so much love to share, so much to look forward to only to have angry men, zealots, using their ignorance and hatred to tear it away from them. He didn't know what she was thinking, didn't even know if she was alive, but he had no indication that she wasn't alive. He couldn't let it go, he had to be here and continue to search, find her or her family, whatever remained.

He fondly remembered the times they spent away in Turkey on the coast or in Istanbul. They had spent long week ends, Atiyah shopping for leather and other supplies for her fathers shop but around this business they carried on a clandestine relationship, sleeping together, getting to know what they could not know in Baghdad. They wandered the shopping areas, buying clothes and trinkets for each other, eating in the restaurants, drinking a glass of wine with dinner, something else she would never be allowed in her neighborhood in Jamilla. It was as if they were married and carrying on an affair, when in fact, they were both single and free to be with each other but in her homeland she would not be allowed this kind of freedom with a single man and especially a Jew in the military. The fact that he was helping her family attempt to resurrect the business allowed him opportunity to be with her but they could not be close or even hold hands. Even the looks they shared could be seen as sinful. But in spite of all this they had found love and found ways to see each other. He remembered back to a time in Istanbul when she was on a leather buying trip for her father. They had met at a small boutique hotel close to the center of town. Many Westerner's came here, from Europe, and the U.S., and many Asian's came here as well. They need have no fear of men or women giving them judgmental stares. They walked the streets with casual abandon and even held hands once in awhile. Back in their room she enjoyed a soak in the huge club foot tub, primping and dressing for him, anticipating his response. Hearing his words of loving praise, seeing in his eyes, love and also desire. This he now fondly remembered as he felt himself become hard with desire. He so wanted her again. Remembrance of long, sensuous love with hands, lips, eyes exploring each other leading to climaxes he knew she never dreamed possible. Also the power she learned she had to control him, teasing, nibbling, bringing him to the brink and then halting, a tease that ended with an even more powerful climax that made his body shutter and collapse in her arms.

He slept fitfully now as the AC hummed in the window and the first calls to prayer, the Azan, could be heard across the city.

CHAPTER EIGHT

8:10 PM, September 16, 2011

Daly City, California

She sat in her small office area in her condo at her computer doing what she did so often when she was alone, search for her family and for David. She had become good at finding search engines that were specific to her needs. She used websites generated by Muslim groups, both here in the states and overseas. She had no reason to believe her brother was dead but no reason to believe otherwise so she searched any site that might give her a contact back to her neighborhood. Recently she found a source on a blog set up by a woman, Saria, from Baghdad, who lived close to where her family had resided. Atiyah had posted a comment to the woman asking if she ever heard from or knew anyone from her street. Today she read with excitement that "Yes, I do have contacts from there and if you would provide names I'll be happy to inquire. This will take some time as you realize this will require a face to face visit as communications with elders is not digital and phones are not yet reliable for most places. Give me a week and hopefully I can get back to you. Please send names you want me to ask about. Enshallah".

Atiyah sent her name, her fathers name, her brothers and a cousin she knew well as a child. Now she needed to wait and see. She dressed in tan shorts, a blue T-shirt, running shoes, grabbing her ear buds and iPod headed out for a run. She headed up to San Francisco State University and ran around the track a few times before continuing around the neighborhood with it's charming bungalows and victorian homes painted in pretty pastels.

CHAPTER NINE

7:30 PM, September 18, 2011

Daly City, California

A few days later, getting home from work and again sitting at her computer, she logged into the website where every day she anxiously awaited some news. She saw there was a message for her and clicking on the icon she read the message from Saria. *Alaikum assalam, I have found your cousin, Shilan, and she is in good health, blessings to Allah, please know she asks of you and your health. I have told her you are fine and living in California and she tells me she has two children now and has married a man from Baghdad. She may have some knowledge of the event you asked about but did not want to talk about it now. She says it was very bad, this thing that happened and she will pray and ask Allah, that she can tell me more. This is all I know now. In the future since you gave me your email address I will send any further information to your email address. Also you may contact me via Skype. May Allah, be with you.*

Atiyah clicked off the message and sent a *"thank you and enshallah to you also."* She sat in front of her computer thinking about what she had read. It was with joy that she now knew her cousin was alive and had children. She hoped she has some happiness from this marriage. Marriage in a Muslim home was almost always arranged and given the number of young men who were driven out of the city with the fighting she was most likely married to an older man. She asked for Allah's blessings for her and went to the kitchen to fix something to eat. She still made meals that reminded her of her home but also had adapted to American style meals. Tonight she would fix a lebanese style salad with grilled eggplant, lettuce, cucumber, nuts, olives and red peppers. As a side dish she had some falafel leftover from the week end.

She was invited to a small party at a fellow nurse's place over in San Francisco, not too far from her place. She didn't have a car, too expensive for parking and not much needed in this city. She showered, picked out a nice black skirt, light weight and full, topped with a black blouse with a sequin design that added a bit of bling to her outfit and then tried several scarves around her waist, settling on a red one. She looked at herself in the mirror and the image brought a memory back of a small room in her father's house, dressing to go out and meet David, only during the day, of course, and always a made up excuse to discuss their case for rebuilding. They could go have tea or coffee at a small cafe around the corner from the Green Zone where David was stationed. She pushed the boundaries of what was acceptable behavior and was often met with stares from the old men in the cafe or even on the street but having lived in the states for several years while getting her degree she was willing to push these boundaries.

Back in the states years before, she had questioned her faith. As she lived in the states longer and got to know others from different backgrounds. She had not lost all her traditional beliefs and only consumed alcohol in social situations, but she did question if Allah or any deity could condemn men and women to Hell for such petty infractions as what was degreed by Mullahs in her homeland. She took a class in religion at the college, in fact that was where she met her first Jew, a young lady from Pittsburgh, Pennsylvania, and became close friends. This had more to do with reshaping her attitudes than anything else. This girl was generous, caring yet was wild and would go out drinking and staying over with young men she met at bars, then come home and tell Atiyah of her nights. It was very distressful to Atiyah but also very stimulating. She would go to her room afterwards and be so sexually excited she would play with herself under her covers and feel guilty afterwards. Finally she felt secure enough in her relationship with "the jewess" as she fondly referred to her friend to ask her to talk to her about sex and boys, as she referred to "them". Eventually she became secure in her own beliefs and felt strong enough to give up her faith, at least as she had known it from her past. She still thought there must be a higher being, but she could see that all "believers" seemed to make up rules and traditions that gave them a false sense of comfort but also set them up to hate others who doubted their beliefs. She decided no God, Allah, or otherwise would require such foolish rules and beliefs. She now took time to consider her life and what was good and what she could do to help others. It was clear her work would be acceptable to any God as good. She also volunteered with a local Muslim community of women who provided help to new immigrants. She was dating a very nice American who treated her like a princess and they had sex, though not as often as he might like, and at least back then, more often than Atiyah was comfortable with. Family values, etc, still clouded her mind and fear of some one spilling the beans made her shy in front of men. She hoped this would pass but still she felt so very free compared to her contemporaries in Iraq. She would never divulge her feelings or admit to having sex to anyone in Iraq. NEVER!

She mingled freely with her fellow nurses and doctors, talked about the events of the day and often shared her family history in Iraq. But even here in her new home she found herself thinking what it would be like if David was here with her and that pushed her thoughts to consider if he was alive and if so where? Would he be looking for her also? This thought was the hardest for her. She did not have a Face Book page, she feared retribution from former militants since she had found out after that terrible event that her own brother was a member of a militant Islamist cell. She still had family there and would not want them to be persecuted for her behavior. She could use the internet but she would not risk as public a place as Face Book. Her colleagues teased her about this but she politely told them she would not be found on FB. She did ask Barb once or twice to let her use her Face Book page and she typed in David's name and came up empty each time.

One of the doctors she worked with came up to her at the party, and asked, "How are you? Have you been able to find any of your family in Iraq? I know you said you had a contact?"

He was about her age, handsome, dark hair, dark complexion, tall and also single, which made her nervous around him. Partly it was her upbringing which allowed men to approach women in her country without embarrassment, while women must always be on guard as to what was expected and who might see this man with her. She was hesitant to put herself out in the single world since her heart was still longing for another, even though she knew it was silly and futile at this point.

Knowing Western men expected eye contact she looked directly at Greg, "Hi Greg! Thanks for asking. I have heard from my contact and I found out I have a cousin alive in my old neighborhood! I am hoping to make contact with her and perhaps I will make a visit back there to see her at some point."

Tilting his head and giving a quizzical glance "Jeez, is it safe enough for you to think about going back there? I'd be too scared!"

"It is reasonably safe now, as I understand it but still you must be aware of your surroundings and of course never go out at night. Well, as a woman, that is a given anyway!"

"I can't imagine how it feels to live under the rules that are imposed on you back there!" Glancing at her empty glass he asks, "Can I get you another glass of wine?"

With a bit of a smile she answers "No, thanks, only one drink! That's it for me. Greg, please understand that for Muslim women, we don't feel as you think we should since we never knew any different. These are not rules as you put it but ways we learned from our elders. Yes, when a man holds power over you and abuses you with that power it hurts and you feel anger, but this is not the case most of the time. Men are usually respectful and shy around women. It is when they marry and take wives that they often become abusive because of our social roles. Men are allowed to believe in their "rights". They believe these rights are given to them in the Quran. Not unlike your bible this is often a matter of interpretation. Now, if I go back home, I would feel different I'm sure. I now know what it is like to be free, as you say. See, in my home back there, I could not, would not, talk to you here. It would be considered shameful behavior and to share a glass of wine would be absolutely not permitted. But you see, I was educated here in the states, as you know, and so I already had been exposed to a different life. When I returned, as was expected by my father, I did have a hard time re-adjusting. My father spoke to me constantly about my behavior and my dressing appropriately. Also, my younger brother, who had become conservative in his beliefs was allowed to preach to me about my role in the home and what "Allah, praise be his name," expected of me." She then looked down and with a small hand gesture and halting words said, "I'm sorry for rattling on about this. I, I hope you don't mind?"

Sitting next to Greg gave her a direct look, "How about we ditch the party, go to the Highland Pub around the corner and have a drink and listen to some jazz?"

Looking up she answers, "Greg, that sounds great but not tonight, I've got some things I need to do on my computer and with time zones here and Iraq it's best for me to do it now. I'm hoping to Skype someone who has contacts with my family there."

"OK, I understand. Maybe another time."

"Yes that would be nice. I'm going to go now. Looking him in the eyes, "Nice seeing you. Good night."

She made her way to the door saying her "Good Byes" as she left. She walked to the Bart station feeling a chill in the night air and after a short ride was home. She dressed for bed, went to her office, turned on the computer and brought up Skype typing in the number her new blogging friend had given her. It was almost mid-night here in California which meant it would be late morning in Baghdad. Skype rang and rang and she was about to give up when her speaker blared out, " *Alaikum assalam my dear Atiyah! Saria, do you have news for me?*"

"*Yes, your cousin is coming over today. I have asked her to come over this afternoon which should make it early Sunday morning for you if that will work? Yes?*"

"Yes, that would be most wonderful! Shukran *dear Saria! I'll wait to hear from you tomorrow!"* She hung up thinking, *"how wonderful this new technology was! She could not only hear Saria but see her and she would see her cousin Shilan tomorrow!* She was so excited but had no one to share this excitement with.

CHAPTER TEN

7:30 AM, September 19, 2011

Daly City, California

Sunday morning and she was dressing in shorts, loose top and running shoes when she heard Skype "ringing" and knew she had a call. Instantly she was excited, hoping this was her cousin Shilan.

She opened her computer and her Skype window, clicking on the phone window box. Immediately she saw a woman she could barely recognize. She spoke in Arabic, "Alaikum assalam, Shilan, that is you!!Oh, it's so good to see you and know you are OK!"

"Yes, Alaikum assalam, my dear cousin I am fine. I have married, it is no one you knew. I am embarrassed but as you may know a single, older women was not desirable after the war started and I had no one to make the necessary arrangements. I was lucky to find a man at all. We have been blessed by Allah, with 2 children. My husband does not have work and that is a problem. I work at a hotel and make a little money but it is hard."

"Oh, I know it must be hard to you." Tears came to Atiyah, thinking of how hard life must be for Shilan. "Please allow me to send some things for you and the children. Does he treat you badly?"

"Most of the time he is fine but he takes his frustrations out on me or the children. I have tried to talk to him but he will not listen and he sometimes turns on me. But I will survive with the help of Allah. Please do not send anything as his pride would be hurt and he would take it out on me."

"Oh, dear Shilan!", her voice breaking, "this war is terrible and even now you are suffering? Yes?"

"Yes, dear Atiyah, it is hard. We have enough to eat most days but electricity is still only a few hours most days. I must plan my meals so cooking is done before we are without and I must keep water in jugs because when there is no electricity there is no water."

"My dear Shilan, how do you cope with getting around? I still hear of so much bombing and there is open hatred between Shia and Shiites, yes?"

"Yes, there are protests in the streets and certain markets, bazaars are not safe to go in. We now live with blast walls around our neighborhoods and we must pass checkpoints, not with U.S. soldiers now, but Iraqi soldiers or police. You can not go anywhere without passing through these and the soldiers are not nice. They will search beneath the clothes of young women, something they would never do under Saddam. It is not safe for women to be out in public alone. I can only go sometimes with the kids but most times I go with my husband for protection."

"What do you know of my brother Siamak?"

"Oh, dear Atiyah! I know he was put in prison after what he did to your friend? David, yes? He got out a few years ago and I have not heard anything about where he is now. Sorry."

"It's Ok, I just wonder if he is alive and well and I feel anger and sadness concerning him."

"Shilan, I am planning on coming to visit you and the kids. Will this be good for you?"

"Oh, it would be wonderful to see you here but it is still dangerous in places. I don't know if that is a good idea, my dear Atiyah?"

"I have thought about it many days now and I know there is danger but it is time for me to go back and settle some things. I will get tickets for next month and I will call and let you know when I will be arriving. Do not worry, I will take a cab from the airport and I am fine with sleeping on the floor or the sofa."

"Atiyah, I am excited to think I could see you again after all these years but you must take care. Do not stop anywhere along the way and do not tell anyone you are originally from Kurdistan, there is so much hatred now between, Shia, Sunni, and Kurds, you can not trust any or them." I wish, so many times now that I could leave this place."

"I will help you if you want to come here to the states. It is so nice where I live, there are trees and flowers everywhere and a woman can walk around anytime safely. It would be a good place for you. We have a large Muslim population not far from here."

With sadness in her voice Shilan responds, "Dear, Atiyah, despite my wishes, I could not leave here, I still have some family and now with my husband, this is not possible. You are dear to think of me. If you wish to come and visit we would welcome you.

I know you understand you must sleep on the floor but we have rugs you can use and we would find food enough for you."

"Shilan I will say good bye and send my love to you and the girls. For now alaikum assalam! We will meet soon. I will send details when I am ready to travel."

They said tearful "Goodbyes" and Atiyah closed Skype and took some time to consider how she might make this trip. She had plenty of vacation time coming from the hospital and she now had a U.S. passport but she would need shots, and would need to have someone take care of her plants. But she knew she had to do this, she needed to make contact with her only remaining family, at least as far as she knew, her brother Siamak might be alive. She wanted to ask about the tragedy that forced her, her father and David out of Baghdad. Worst of all for her was the questions about her brother. She needed to know his involvement and where was he now? Also she had so many questions about David and what happened to him?

The next couple of weeks were busy with appointments to get shots, check with the embassy to see about any visa problems, time on the internet seeking advice on getting from the airport into town,etc,etc. She had almost 35 hours to spend in the air or in airports, on toTurkey overnight and into Baghdad in the early morning. She would bring a couple of books, her kindle, which she had no idea if it would work, and her iPhone. It was going to be a long haul.

She remembered the rushed flights out of Baghdad after David was rescued, when she was much younger, but those were military flights to Germany and then a commercial flight to the U.S.. It was hard on her father but the military and commercial flight attendants were so gracious and knew the circumstances of why they were being flown to the U.S.. After the kidnapping and rescue, Atiyah was allowed to make a request for visas for her and her father to leave Iraq as refugees, due to extreme danger from enemy combatants. She thought back to that day when she was in the shop, still badly damaged from the Allied bombing. She was going over the plans with her father for the rebuilding of his shop. They had drawn up the plans with help from David and his staff. Suddenly the door was pushed open and six marines in full combat dress, rushed in with weapons drawn and told them in Arabic to get down on the floor. Her poor father hesitated and one soldier stepped forward and pushed him roughly down on the floor while the others quickly moved through the crumbled remains of their shop and living areas. Searching the house, obviously looking for evidence of Siamak and his cellmates having been there, and found nothing, they told Atiyah and her father to grab some clothes and prepare to stay overnight or longer.

When she protested she was told "get some clothes for you and your father or you'll be removed without any. Your choice lady! We have our orders and you will need to hurry."

"But why? And what happened to Captain Goldman?" Now panic began to set in and she began shaking. "What happened!! Where is he? I'm not going anywhere until I know what has happened to him!! Please don't do this to me! I need to know!" With this she began to sob, shaking with fear of what was unknown. "Mam, I don't know anything about Captain Goldman, I only know what my orders are: bring you to a safe location where you will be met by someone from the embassy. I can only assume they will be able to tell you more. Now let's go."

She grabbed what she could, put the clothes for herself and her father in a cloth suitcase and they stood before the soldiers, heads bowed in resignation. They were hustled into a waiting military

Humvee and taken through the checkpoint into the green zone, formerly the site of Saddam's palaces and now the entire area behind blast walls and a bastion of American and Allied power. Escorted to a small house and told to make themselves at home but do not try to leave, Atiyah tried to ask if they were under arrest and if so on what charges? The soldiers did not answer but left, leaving another soldier guarding the door.

Shortly a woman who spoke perfect Arabic came to the door and asked if they would like food and water. She apologized but could answer no more than the soldiers and went away bringing back food, water and tea. Hours later an officer came to talk to them and told them what had happened with David. She asked if David was alright and the officer would not comment on that and was only here to tell them the operation to rescue David was successful. Because of the circumstances surrounding her and her father the American embassy would be coming to talk to them. Now this was a surprise just as much as all the other actions of this day.

The Embassy Counsel came to see them telling them they would provide a temporary visa for her father and of course she still had her student visa. If they accepted the offer, they would be transported to the states in the morning. This was unbelievable to Atiyah! What had happened to David? Where was he? What had caused the U.S. embassy to get involved? The Embassy Counsel explained that the involvement of Al Qaeda and likely her brother, the fact that they knew about the family connection to Captain Goldman and possibly an inappropriate relationship assured that they were a target for retribution. Since Atiyah had a passport she was being offered a one way trip back to the states and her father would be allowed a guest visa. If they refused the offer to leave there would be no further protection offered. Her father heard all of this but could not comprehend what was going on and refused to believe his daughter was in any way involved with the American Captain.

Atiyah was left with the difficult job of convincing her father they must leave or they would be killed by his own people. Further that his son Siamak was found to be a part of the kidnapping of the American captain. He stopped listening to Atiyah and withdrew into himself. Atiyah spent hours going over the choices, though it seemed like they only had one choice since staying and waiting for a bomb to kill them or a rain of bullets in the street mowing them down did not seem like a choice worth taking. Hours later when the embassy representative came back she told him, with resignation, "Yes, we will go to the states." They were provided orders from the American embassy, and an embassy staff liaison worked to get them expedited treatment. Military intelligence had marked the family as *"in danger from insurgents"* since Atiyah and her father had been cooperating with the U.S. military and other U.S. personnel attempting to repair their business since the bombing. Atiyah knew now that the Marines suspected her brother was involved in an al Qaeda cell and the kidnapping of David.

They were offered financial assistance to re-establish themselves in the states. They had to spend a week in Germany at the military base, getting and shots, filling out paperwork for her father, etc before being flown to San Francisco where they were greeted by a representative of the Muslim community. This man became very helpful to them and the community was a tremendous help in finding temporary housing, knowing how to get around, finding medical care for her ailing father who continued to not believe what they told him. He went along, pride broken, head down and now depleted of life, a bag of old bones waiting for Allah to call him home.

When she thought back to those days, it filled her with sadness and longing. Sadness for loss of her dear father, it was only 2 years from the time they arrived when he suffered a massive stroke and he only lasted 6 months before passing. She was left alone, burying her father in a strange land, but with help from the community and her ability to find work at the hospital she found new friends and quickly adapted to her new home in Daly city, only a short ride away from her work at UCSF Medical.

CHAPTER ELEVEN

8:00 AM, October 20, 2011

Daly City, California

Another spring like day, even thought it was fall, most days in this city reminded Atiyah of spring in Baghdad, cool and crisp. Walking into the hospital, greeting staff she knew and as usual finding Barb in the locker room, getting ready to start the day.

"Hey sister! Wuz up??"

She still had a laugh with these American sayings that were not standard English as she knew it, and often caught her off guard.

"Hey sister! Busy, busy, getting myself ready for my big trip! How you doing with the house hunting?"

"Crazy! But if we don't take advantage of this market, we'll regret it so we keep looking. Lots of short sales, you know, but you have to wait, and wait for the bank to work through the process only to find they reject your offer and you have to start over! We put in an offer again this week end, nice place over by Mission.

Just have to wait and see. No changing your mind on this crazy trip?? I worry for your safety!"

"Puuleez! I won't be there all that long and my cousin knows where it's safe to travel. Relax! I know the trip in from the airport will be the worst part for me. It's so sad to me to see my city torn apart by this violence and now with the U.S. pulling out I can only see it getting worse. I hope I can convince my cousin to leave. She is of Kurdish descent and with these crazies controlling who comes and goes and who should die she may be in real danger. Her husband is Sunni, which where we lived was a good thing but you can't rely on that when you must leave and go into the markets or to a medical clinic. So I will go and see what I can do. Try to convince her to come back with me."

"And I know you are still hoping to find some hint of what happened to David? Huh?"

With a shrug and big sigh, "Oh God, yeah! I suppose so, I'd like to know....., one way or the other." She finished pulling her scrubs on, looked at Barb and started to walk out.

"OK, time to get to work! See you on the floor!"

The day passed quickly and Atiyah hopped on BART and then got off at the U.S. Embassy and after sitting in line for 45 minutes sat down with a clerk who examined her papers, Visa, etc, and told her she was all set, no questions should come up at security and she also should be fine with processing into Iraq, though she was told the actual process was out of their control now.

She had gone to the clinic in her hospital and they had checked her past vaccination history and only a typhoid shot was required. Now with everything in place she looked forward to her trip next week. She still had some apprehensions and the clerk at the Embassy had warned her to be vigilant and not to go out alone, even during the day.

CHAPTER TWELVE

7:00 AM, October 20, 2011

Baghdad, Iraq

David was out the door of his apartment and his escort car was waiting. The day was going to be hot, again! The sky was white as most days, dust blurred the blue into blazing white heat. It was cool in the morning but would be 90 by noon and 110 degrees by 5 PM. The car was provided by DWB for security reasons. It appeared to be a junker, 10 years old, dusty and in need of a paint job, but it was refitted with a very powerful BMW engine and drive train with sports car suspension and tires. The doors had extra strong kevlar inserts that would stop most bullet. He hoped he'd never need the protection but it was nice knowing it was there. His driver, Jamal, waved and said, "Sabah el kheer, (good morning in Arabic) along with the customary "alaikum assalam". They were going to a meeting at a new medical clinic site to check on construction. It was about 30 minutes away but in Baghdad that could be 2 hours or more, if there were problems on the streets. As they traveled the dusty streets, concrete or stucco buildings lined both sides of the road and many windows were broken and chunks of concrete were blown from buildings where bombs or bullets had hit them. They approached a checkpoint. Jamal rolled down the window and the dusty warm air of October floated in as David handed over his passport and ID from DWB. The policeman scrutinized both his papers and Jamal's then told him there was a problem with the street ahead and it would be best to take an alternate route. Jamal said "Thank you" in Arabic and they went one block and turned left as instructed. All was fine until they got about 3 miles down and out of nowhere a car flew out from a side street and stopped across the road not allowing them to pass. The door of the old beat up green Mercedes burst open and a man wearing a camouflaged jacket and traditional dishdasha jumped out with a rifle pointed at David and Jamal. "Here we go again!" said David rolling his eyes in frustration. One man, dressed in scruffy camouflage fatigues came up to Jamal and asked what his business was in this part of town. Jamal explained that he was driving David to a meeting for a new clinic. When the man heard this he laughed and turned to look at David. In Arabic he said to Jamal, "This man is a U.S. CIA agent! No! Why do you have anything to do with him? He looked at David with anger and yellow stained teeth barred and yelled, "What the fuck do you think you are doing in our land? Who the fuck do you think you are! You fucking Infidel! There is no clinic! We no need help!" David turned his head, looked away with impatience, put his hands out in a calm down gesture, trying to calm the man. He understood enough Arabic and protested that he was in fact building a clinic and he had the necessary papers to prove it. The man only became more intense and shouted, "You Americans come here, blow up our country, turn U.S. one against the other and now you want to claim you are helping us! Are you stupid??"

David said calmly, "I work for Doctors Without Borders, we are a French NGO (non-government organization)and are here to help restore your medical infrastructure. We are not political and I ask you to let U.S. pass. You may call Amhed Mohamad he will verify what we are doing." He gave the number to Jamal who handed it out the window to the gunman. The man pulled out a cell phone and called the number. After a long drawn out phone conversation,it was clear from the tone of voice the man was talking to someone who demanded respect. The gunman put the phone away, turned to David and with downcast eyes said, "I apologize sir, you may proceed, alaikum assalam" The man kicked at the car tire and jumped back into his car.

Just as quickly as they had come the car flew away, leaving Jamal and David sitting in a cloud of dust with cars piled up behind honking at them to move, which they were more than happy to do. David tried to calm down but this was one more reminder why this place was becoming increasingly dangerous for him and the organization.

The rest of the trip went fine and they arrived at a yellow stucco one story building which looked new, had new trim around the windows and a sign hanging over the door Jamiya Health Clinic in Arabic. Jamal, his driver for the last two years, was wiry, dark, scraggly hair, and an infectious smile that he beamed at almost anyone who approached him. But he took his job seriously, and before David exited the car, Jamal looked up and down the street for signs of trouble and across the street at the blown apart building. When he deemed all was clear he got out and opened the door for David to exit. As they entered they were greeted by the workers who were finishing up details and painting ready to call the job done and turn it over to DWB. David's job was liaison between contractors and DWB and now he needed to check on last minute details and continue to plan for the delivery of medical equipment and supplies that were sitting in a warehouse. Even this gesture of a clinic that most people would assume would be accepted with enthusiasm was under constant threat from extremist such as those who had waylaid them this morning.

After his inspection of this clinic he asked Jamal to drive to another clinic recently opened a few miles away. Once again Jamal went through back roads to avoid checkpoints which not only slowed progress but were focal points for bombs or attacks. They reached the other clinic, only 30 minutes away normally, after over an hour of evasive driving on streets filled with gaping holes from mortar or bombs that were badly filled in by local men, and squeaking through narrow streets pinched tight with stalls selling everything from tea to groceries parked right on the street. Many stores had not been repaired or opened and these stalls took up the slack but made it difficult to drive any distance.

David went in the clinic, which like the new one he was currently working on was a bright, airy space inviting to families. Walls in the reception area were painted by local artists with murals of families and children playing. He moved through the reception area feeling the eyes of women with children who knew he was not one of them if not a foreigner. An old man glanced at him also as he went down the hallway to the office where a woman got up from her desk as she saw him enter, "Ahh, Mr. White, Good morning, oh, sorry good day to you! I see it is almost lunch time! How can I help you?"

"Alaikum assalam, Zara, it is so nice to see you again! I wanted to talk to you and see if everything is going well and if the other supplies we ordered had come in?"

"Yes, almost everything is here now. I'm missing some meds but they should be here any day. We are busy with wounds to tend to, it is hard to see so many burns, severe abrasions, some we would not treat here but there is little choice since, as you know the hospital is overwhelmed."

"And what of women abused? Are the numbers getting better?", questioned David.

"Yes, the numbers are down but it is still such a tragedy to know that men who claim to honor Allah, can treat a woman so badly! It is something that would not happen before the war. So many men have left their women and gone off to join some jihad group and those men who run in groups here claiming to be part of jihad will find a woman walking the streets without a man and assault her, rape her and tell her it is her fault for being without a man. What kind of sense is this? It is an excuse they use to do what they want. And in the name of Allah!"

"These are men who have lost their vision of good and need to control others to convince themselves of their righteousness. Alaikum assalam dear Zara. I must be on my way. Please call the office if your supplies do not come in by the end of the week. Doctor Jamison is working out well? Yes?"

Yes, she is great and we could use ten more like her! Thank you so much for all you do!"

You are very welcome. See you!"

David pulled out his cell and called Jamal to tell him he was coming out in two minutes and to pick him up at the curb.

Jamal was there and they wound their way back to his apartment. Jamal checked the rearview mirror before letting him exit and they checked schedules for tomorrow as David exited and walked up the stairs to his apartment.

As he sat in his courtyard sipping a glass of wine, something he could not do in public, he was feeling that longing in his heart, that stone that he turned and turned, wearing it smooth but still the memories lingered, he wondered how she was and where she was? Finally a different hunger called and he went about making supper and calling it a day.

CHAPTER THIRTEEN

5:31 AM, October 23, 2011

San Francisco Airport lounge

Atiyah had been up early taking care of last minute needs and then hopped onto Bart, the light rail train that took her out to the airport. She was there early waiting for her flight to Istanbul and on to Baghdad. Atiyah was dressed conservatively in black, knowing she would not want to draw attention to herself when she arrived in Baghdad some 30 plus hours from now. Her thoughts after take off, as she sat in a window seat trying to nap at 37,000 feet, were on how her cousin would look and how the city would be so different now after all the war had done. Streets barricaded, wreckage of blown up cars littering the roads as if some kind of metal sculptures. She knew this as many in the U.S. did from watching too much of CNN footage on TV. She had many hours to dwell on her past, her possible future, on David, and on her cousin. Eventually sleep overcame her and she woke to the flight attendants readying the plane for landing in Istanbul.

Arriving in Istanbul at 11 AM, she had a long layover. Her flight to Baghdad would leave at 6 AM the next day. She hailed a cab at the curb and went to her hotel. Now being a single woman here, was not a problem in multicultural Istanbul but she knew she would get the hard looks from the cab drivers when she was in Baghdad. She had hoped so much when the war started that women would find the strength to stand up for their rights but it had so far, not happened. For now she went to her room walking through the lobby decorated in old Byzantine style with plenty of gold leaf on lovely wood borders framing primitive scenes of life in old Turkey. Lovely blue and deep red colors and the walls festooned with old Persian carpets. The floor of marble tile also had lovely tribal rugs that she admired and made her think of her own Persian carpets at home.

Walking through the hustle and bustle of downtown Istanbul she wandered the bazaar shops inspecting the leather goods, comparing them to her fathers work. Running her hand over the smooth leather, dyed reddish brown and fine stitching done by strong hands, probably a family business. At a stall she bought herself a couple of silk scarfs to wear around Baghdad, in case she had a chance to go out to a nice restaurant, if there was any safe enough to allow her to be there. She walked by the spice markets piled high with colorful spices and herbs redolent with the smells of the Orient, cardamon,curries of all kinds, peppercorns, garlic, huge piles of dried peppers. More strange smells she could not identify assailed her nose in pungent and pleasant ways . A few shops away she came across glass oil lamps in gorgeous colors, hanging like the tear drops from a rainbow and then she passed the little cafe where she and David had previously sipped tea or coffee early in the morning and later in the day a glass of wine with small plates of Greek, or Tunis, or Lebanese foods, lovely to smell and delicious to eat. These memories brought back lovely times and tears welled in her eyes as she watched other couples sitting at small tables deep in chit chat or just holding hands.

All these behaviors in public were something tolerated and open here in this cosmopolitan city on the Bosporus Strait but they would not be tolerated in Baghdad, especially now that the Shia and Sunni were at each others throats. Since she had experienced the freedom of the West she wanted so much to see her homeland become more like this wonderful city, inclusive but tolerant. She would like muslims to see that they could believe as they wish but not try to force others to believe the same. She saw much to like in the Muslim faith but also in all the major religions. It did not honor your religion to have it shoved down some one else's throat. If your religion is so precious others will see this for themselves.

It was late afternoon and after a light but tasty dinner in one of the cafes she headed back to her hotel and with a book on the history of Istanbul in her lap spent the last couple of hours reading before heading to bed and preparing for the last leg of her long journey in the morning. She She awoke around midnight jet lagged, thinking of David and the times they had been here in Istanbul. The long days with many hours of making love and being loved. The fun of walking the streets, going to shows, window shopping and then late evenings finding their favorite little cafe by the water. Coming back to their room, she would go take a long bath, soak in perfumed water, put on a long silk robe and with a dash of Turkish perfume in just the right places slink under the bed covers and meet David's waiting lips and much more! Her smile and the warmth between her thighs soon led to sweet dreams.

Dawn came too early and she grabbed a cab to the airport. After processing through security sat at a cafe inside close to her gate and had coffee and a Turkish sweet bread. She boarded on time and with some nervousness took her window seat and as the plane climbed steeply watched the twinkling lights of the minarets slide below her and fade away as they cruised over the deep blue of the Mediterranean sea.

CHAPTER FOURTEEN

9:15 AM, October 25, 2011

Baghdad, Iraq

David was off today, and had plans to visit his friend Paul Burkhart who had been stationed with him when he was in service here. Paul operated a private security service and was doing very well. He had the best security money could buy and owned condos in Miami, Istanbul, and London where his business was headquartered.

He entered the little cafe not far from his place and spotted Paul sitting in a corner with tea waiting for him. Paul got up and they hugged and greeted each other warmly, "Hey Paul! How are you? What's going on? Haven't heard from you in awhile?"

Paul pushed back and gave David the once over, "David, you look good! Great to see you also! Busy man, busy! And it's all good! Sit down! Have some tea or let me get you a coffee? Nice weather huh? After the heat of summer these cool days feel great."

"Coffee yes, tea no, still not quite a native I guess, and yes, I like the weather. Turned my AC off last few days! So tell me what's going on in the security world?"

"It's crazy huh? I'm making 5 times as much as I was in Marines! But it's still dangerous here! Let me tell you! But at least we have some of the best equipment money can buy and I continue to enjoy the travel this job allows me. I spend a lot of time in London now you know, working on my computer, putting together contracts but still I find time to enjoy the city. I also stop in Paris for a week or so and along the way back I often stop in Munich or Istanbul. I keep saying I have a 5 year plan, but that was 5 years ago!"

"Paul, you amaze me!"

"Yes, well same to you! I see you're still here with DWB and living outside the wall! Not as dangerous as before but still chancy! What ever happened with that woman you were involved with? What was her name?"

"Atiyah! I don't know anything about what happened with her, in fact I was hoping to ask you if you could do a little sleuthing for me? I enjoy my work here and, like you, keep believing things will improve. Hey, back to Atiyah! Could you see what comes up in your little crystal ball?"

"Oh! you want me to see if I can find anything on your little Islamist princess? You'll have to give me all you can on her family, former address, etc. I'll see what I can do. I have some good people working for me here and in London, they should be able to find something. On things improving here? I'm more skeptical than ever. The violence between Shia and Sunni just gets worse and frankly makes my job that much harder."

They spent time rehashing events from the past when they were both assigned to the Marine corps here in Iraq and Paul told him that after the kidnapping he found out some things that maybe David didn't want to know. He explained that his sources told him Atiyah's brother was known to be a member of an active Al Qaeda cell and there was evidence pointing to involvement in the kidnapping. In fact Siamak had been captured with David and sent off to a prison in Iraq where he subsequently escaped two years later.

David went away from their meeting with some anger thinking about what he had learned. He had suspected Atiyah's brother was likely involved in his kidnapping! Now he knew it! Shit that really pissed him off! Where was the bastard now? David had not ask Paul to look into that but now called Paul, got his voice mail, left a message asking him to look into Siamak's current doings.

CHAPTER FIFTEEN

10:26 AM, October 26, 2011

Baghdad, Iraq

Paul called his London office and after taking care of his usual business issues he asked his main *"go to computer geek"* Joel to check out Atiyah Rashid and family. "Find out what you can, check here in Iraq, and in the States. Also see what you can come up with on her brother Siamak, same last name as far as I know. Had affiliation with terrorists groups here in Iraq and was involved in kidnapping of a U.S. Marine back in '05. The Marine was David Goldman and you should be able to find a report on that kidnapping from 3rd Battalion 4th Marine Squadron. Get back to me with whatever you find ASAP. Thanks, Joel." He hung up and sat there for minute wondering what his buddy David was going to do with this info? It could also lead Paul into a situation he wasn't sure he wanted to be in. If he found Siamak was still with a cell he couldn't just pass on that info to David. He was in a position to protect his countrymen, even if this info was requested by a private individual, not the military, he wouldn't knowingly let an Al Qaeda cell operate in this city, either against Americans, or citizens of Baghdad, or maybe another attempt on his buddies life. *Well, let's see where this trail leads and then decide, he thought.*

His company provided security for oil rigs, infrastructure, private individuals, foreign companies and their executives. They provided training for threats that may appear when driving the dangerous roads of Iraq. They provided vehicles, such as the one David used, from old looking cars with high end mechanical systems to high end cars such as Mercedes, BMW's or Land Rovers with extreme security packages. It was a lucrative business and Paul loved the excitement, though he had also lost quite a few friends and employees along the way.

CHAPTER SIXTEEN

3:46 PM, October 27, 2011

Jamilla, Iraq

She had been picked up at the Baghdad International Airport, previously known as Saddam International Airport, by a cab and given a cool reception by the cab driver. She gave directions and found her way to her cousins place, only blocks from where her own family had lived.

Her cousin had screamed hysterically when she exited the cab and presented herself at the door.

"Atiyah! Atiyah! Alaikum assalam, alaikum assalam! I am so excited to see you in the flesh at my humble door! Please let me get your bags and bring you inside!!"

They entered a small crowded courtyard that barely qualified as such. A scrawny cat ran for cover as they entered, two bedraggled kids came over wrapping themselves around their mothers skirt.

"Amira! Shada! Stand still and let ana-sahbti, your cousin see you! What do you say?"

Amira said, "Hello. My name is Amira." in English, with a shy smile and looking down at her feet, clad in dirty sandals.

"Shada! What do you say?"

"Alaikum assalam, I am Shada. I am eleven years old."

"Come on, now you can say the rest."

"And it is nice to meet you." As she made a little hop and her face lit up with a big smile!

As Atiyah hugged Shilan she sighed, "It is so good to see you! And to meet your children! It has been a long trip but everything went fine, even the ride from the airport but it is so sad to see all the damage and the ugly blast walls everywhere. I do not know how you can live this way my dear cousin?"

"Oh, it is what it is and in the hands of Allah. Sorry dear cousin, please come in, put your bags against the back wall. As you can see we do not have a lot of room but we will make the couch up for you to sleep on."

They moved through the little front room, crowded with a small stove, sink and some simple cupboards painted in Persian designs. One wall held shelves with some books and close by there was a rug hanging from the ceiling pulled aside by a cord and it was clear this area was a bedroom and a sleeping bag was rolled up and set against the wall. Another rug held in the same way closed off another area. *"Wow! This is how they live! I don't know if I could do this anymore! I am so spoiled now!"* She thought to herself not wanting to hurt Shilan's feelings. They sat on the couch and talked about family, her job, what it was like to live in the states and Shilan talked a little about her life and the kids attempts to go to school. School was not good and many days they were sent home because the teacher was sick or too scared to come to school because of threats.

As they were sitting with the kids giving her rapt attention someone came into the courtyard, moved about out there and then slid through the door gazing down at the floor. He stood there looking at Shilan and said in Arabic, "Wife, who is this woman that has entered my home?"

Shilan speaks softly with downcast eyes, "Alaikum assalam dear husband, this is my cousin I have told you of before. Her family lived here in our neighborhood years ago. You may remember her father, Muamar, who owned the leather shop? I had asked your permission for her to stay for only a few days, dear husband."

He gave a slight welcome shrug of his shoulders with the usual utterance, "If Allah wishes" and retired, slinking like a shadow to the little back room where Atiyah could hear a TV playing news from Aljazeera.

Later the family has retired to the back room, Atiyah imagines them in the room, all together on a rug with a shared ragged blanket for cover. She herself has the same, though knowing her cousin, hers would be the best they have. She lies here, in the dark, having heard the Al-isha floating from the minaret outside the mosque and having prostrated herself with the family, her cousin's husband alone in front and she, her cousins in back reciting the prayers from the Quran. Her memories now drift back to her family, her father, living not far from here. The last few years before all the trouble, when her father would take her hand and walk down to the river and sit on a bench with her and tell her of his life, his losses, his triumphs. She can feel his calloused hands, hands that turned the rough leather into beautiful objects. She can smell the leather, the oil on his clothes and takes all this in just as if she was there at his side listening to him recite his stories, stories she has heard often. These are not her memories but they are now wrapped in her memories, like layers of the Iraqi flat bread, khubz she can pull them apart and find memories of her father in between the layers. Now, here with all the familiar sounds, smells, she smiles sweetly for her father who would say to her, *"Dear Atiyah, listen and remember who we are, where we came from, what we did, so that long after I have passed you will know who you are also."*

CHAPTER SEVENTEEN

6:38 PM,November 5th, 2011,

Kurdistan, Iraq

Taariq sat on the dirt floor of the small, squat house in this dusty, bedraggled village in Northern Kurdistan, even the mosque was tired looking with a minaret sadly short in stature, with a rickety wooden staircase for the local muezzin to climb and call out adhan or prayers. This village outside of Kurkuk, had suffered from the invasion like much of Iraq and was a mixed bag of dilapidated houses mixed in with some shops, a mosque, all done in a dirt brown color allowing the town to blend in with the desert. Taariq was brooding over the intel they had received from Jamilla. He was young, skinny, dark and had little formal education but had a burning desire to rid his country of the infidels. Taariq had taken command of this cell from Abida who had beem moved to another outpost. No one stayed long with a cell since this made it much harder for the authorities to track them down. He had brought Siamak back in to the cell after he escaped from jail and now it was time for Siamak to make the ultimate sacrifice. Taariq still was not convinced Siamak had the true calling. Taariq had come with a plan to bring respect back to Simak's family with an honor killing and the mullah had listened to his reasons and approved, saying it was justified and supported by Mohammed's word.

Siamak, Atiyah's brother, had passed on information from his cousin Shilan's husband in Jamilla. Their cell brother Faaris, was here with them now, telling them they had received the go ahead from their comrades in Baghdad to kidnap Siamak's sister and make an example of her to other women who may consider dishonoring the family by fraternizing with an infidel. The American Jew captain who was now suspected of being a spy working for Doctors Without Borders in Baghdad had also again become a target but first they would deal with Siamak's sister. Siamak had passed on intel that his sister, Atiyah was back, visiting her cousin Shilan, also in Baghdad.

Faaris spoke in a low gravelly voice with implied distrust, "I do not trust Siamak's sources. I understand he received this intel from the husband of his cousin. This man may or may not be reliable. We must press him for assurances on this information being reliable. We will need to move forward soon with our plans to bring justice and honor to our cause and praise to Allah. We have received word to proceed with a kidnapping and use of his sister Atiyah and Siamak as martyr's. I will seek assurances from Siamak on this matter tomorrow, and with Allah's blessing we will move our plans forward one week from today."

CHAPTER EIGHTEEN

3:23 PM, November 6, 2011

Kurdistan, Iraq

Faaris rises from the prayer rug in this small, squat house and lowers his head in greeting to Siamak. "Alaikum assalam dear brother Siamak. And has Allah given you the courage to speak to us of your sister in Jamilla and of the infidel?"

"Alaikum assalam my brother! I am told by my cousin's husband in Jamilla, my sister, Atiyah has returned and is staying with them there. May she rot in Hell for befriending this American Jew! Atiyah is in Jamilla now with our cousin but I do not know of any contact now with the American Jew Goldman. Shilan's husband tells me this man now calls himself Daniel White. The husband suspects he may be spying for the Americans. I am determined to bring back respect and honor to our family name. She must be punished for her past sins and stopped before she again dishonors the Rashid family name. I will, with heavy heart bring retribution down on her, for the family and for the Muslim brotherhood. Give me the word and I will go to Jamilla and carry out these plans."

"This is good Siamak, but remember the last time we kidnapped the Jew, there was a leak somewhere and we lost two brothers, may they be with Allah. We can not afford that again. There are some who believe you may have been the leak, with or without your knowledge. Do you understand brother?"

"Yes, but be clear that I was not at fault in that failed attempt. I know not what went wrong but with Allah's blessing I did my part and never broke my vows. The Americans have very good spies and resources to listen to our talk and it must be this that provided them with our plans."

"Siamak, your role now is to go back to Jamilla and set up a safe house and bring in the supplies we need. We will give you further orders for the completion of your brave act when all is in place. We will work to snatch the infidel at another time. We will bring him back here for the final video and blessing with the beheading as planned. Your sister will go with you to be martyred and both of you will meet Allah in heaven. Go now and prepare! May Allah be with you."

Siamak speaks softly with eyes downcast, with his hands clasped in prayer, "I have prayed on this for many days now! I am ready! I will be with Allah very soon, may He be blessed forever."

Now in a clear strong voice he says, "I have the throw away phone and will use it only as instructed with the code you have provided. I will go, sacrifice myself and meet Allah! I will restore honor to the Rashid family name which my sister has besmirched!"

"Siamak, this is good! Allah will receive you as a brave and honorable Muslim! Your reward shall be with Allah! Alaikum assalam" He bows to Siamak and dismisses him.

CHAPTER NINETEEN

8:10 AM, November 11, 2011

Jamilla, Iraq

Siamak travels to Jamilla and in less than a week, using an alias obtains a safe house and the necessary supplies for the operation.

He uses the throwaway phone to call Faaris, "Alaikum assalam, brother I have all we need and you are welcome to visit any time. Please let me know your arrival when plans are finalized." This was all he said and then closed the phone, not even waiting for an answer. He would take one call from Faaris as to their arrival and then the phone would be used as a detonator for an IED if needed. Siamak had made up his mind and prayed every day for Allah to bless him and choose him to enter heaven with his sister. The plan at first was a kidnapping, with a beheading, but Siamak with Faaris' guidance, had decided to make the ultimate sacrifice and bring his sister and himself to Allah's door in heaven. The infidel would be dealt with also but not with his sister. The Jew would be kidnapped later and brought to Kurdistan for a video and beheading. Siamak did feel badly that he would not be alive to see this but was accepting of his role and his bringing honor back to his family name.

To himself, *"I do regret that I have not seen my sister before she is kidnapped and executed. This is the only member of my family alive and I should spend some time with her before she is sent on her way to Allah, if he so desires."* He wished Atiyah and his father had never been involved with the Americans. He had come back from Kirkuk a few times and pleaded with his father to not go to the Americans for their blood money but his father refused to listen. Then to make matters worse he used Atiyah to interpret for him, even though the Americans had offered an interpreter. He was not there when these meetings took place or when supposedly Atiyah was seen meeting with the American Jew but his comrades had informed him that she was seen on numerous occasions with this man, though no touching took place, the sources indicated their eyes betrayed them. This would never be tolerated by his comrades or the males in his family if they learned of it. He felt anger for being placed in this position by Atiyah. He would never think of hurting his sister but this was now an issue of honor and he would be seen as weak if he did not exact punishment of her and retribution on the Jew. He also recalled the long days sitting in the dark cold, windowless cell of an Iraqi jail when the soldiers pulled him from the house where the kidnapping took place. The trial by the new Iraqi government council was a sham and after 2 years in a filthy so called prison he escaped. He was malnourished but alive and with help from local al-Qaeda he returned north to Kirkuk.

Now here just, outside Jamilla, in the safe house they had found with help from local Al-Qaeda cell, Siamak could not sleep and with early morning showing slits of light around the shaded windows he brooded over what to do about his dear sister. He got up from his prayer rug as he heard the first call to prayer settle over the city like the soft cooing of a dove landing in the courtyard. He prostrated himself towards Mecca and prayed to Allah for guidance. When he was finished it had come to him that he owed his dear sister a chance to be confronted and charged with her immoral acts and to beg Allah forgiveness before vengeance was delivered.

CHAPTER TWENTY

1:56 PM, November 12, 2011

Jamilla,Iraq

A couple of days after her arrival in Jamilla, Shilan mentioned to Atiyah, "I have some friends who would like to meet you and if you would like we will go there tonight and have some food, tea, talk and enjoy the company of other women. Would you like to do this?"

"Really? I'd love it! I remember times like this when I was young. It was a comfort for the women to know they were not being judged by men and they could just relax and gossip or whatever. Ok, let's do it!"

Later they arrive at a home, much nicer than where Shilan lives, with the girls in tow and are welcomed into a lovely home. The hostess, Jada greets them and shows them around the home which has carpets on the floors in every room and artwork on the walls. It is late afternoon and shafts of sunlight fill the room with warmth, there is Persian music playing, large pillows around the perimeter of the large room and a couple of low overstuffed couches along two opposing walls. In the center are two round low tables, dark wood and these again are surrounded by pillows. Atiyah takes in the colors of dark reds, yellows, with lots of sequins reflecting light and then picks up the familiar smell of incense in the air. All of this is familiar to her from her childhood and is comforting. Jada introduces her to two other ladies, Na'ima and Labiba. Nai'ma is short and somewhat overweight with long dark curly hair and she is wearing bright dark red print lounge pajamas that would not be out of place in San Francisco. She, as do all the women, has tons of gold bracelets and large gold earrings. Labiba is the opposite, tall, slender, dark skin, short straight dark hair and deep set eyes with a strong Roman nose. She is very striking and she is dressed in black leotards topped with a tight somewhat revealing yellow blouse. She sits with her legs crossed and lights up the room with her eyes and smile. She comes across as from a higher social class, though Shilan never mentioned this when telling her about the group as they walked over. Jada is in between the other two, somewhat curly, medium length dark auburn hair, with an orange top covered with yellow flowing cape-like blouse, and very petty blue and green print scarf at her neck.

After the customary greetings and showing of the home the ladies move back to the central room and take seats around the tables. Jada has Shilan's two girls help her bring tea with porcelain cups and small sweet breads to the tables and then they are all seated.

Jada starts by giving more of an introduction concerning Atiyah and her family. She asks Atiyah if she would mind explaining what her job is in the states and a little about California which is so strange to these ladies.

Atiyah does her best with her unused Arabic to explain her job, how big the hospital is, how many, many women work there and she goes anywhere she likes and never worries about men bothering her. She explains that yes, California is very large and there are many very wealthy people around where she lives but also a lot of people like herself, who can afford only small condos or houses. She quickly becomes the center of the group.

Jada, who seems more assertive than the others asks, "Atiyah tell us about meeting men and how do you do that if no one arranges the meeting." She rolls her eyes and laughs as she says this.

Atiyah answers with a slight grin, finding this naivety charming. "You meet men in the states almost anywhere."

"But surely you would not speak to a man passing on the street?" says Nai-ma with eyes big as saucers.

"No, you could but that would be only because he is in your way or something like that. Of course if you see him and you know him it is proper to say, "Hello" and this might lead to a conversation about meeting for coffee or a dinner sometime. Mostly you would meet a stranger at a coffee shop or in the produce aisle at the grocery store."

Labiba pipes up, "You can just go to a coffee shop and talk to a man and tell him you want to marry him!!" This gets tons of giggles and laughter from the others.

"No! No!" shrieks Atiyah with laughter! "But if he sees you having coffee, alone..."

"Alone! You can not!" laughs Jada! Please Atiyah tell us how this can be??"

Atiyah goes on, "If he sees you have on something very pretty or unique, he may look at you as he passes and comment on how pretty you loo. If you like the way he looks, you could say, with a direct look that invites more talk, "Thank you." or you may give a polite but quick "Thanks" and he will know you're not inviting more talk. I don't always get it yet. Sometimes the signals men and women send are hard to read and I still feel shy. But if you go out with women to a bar or to dinner, a man may pass by that some one in the group knows and he may be invited to stop and talk or have a drink. This is when introductions take place and if you want you can give the man your card or cell number."

They all shriek again at this, "Give him your cell number! Oh blessed Allah! Never! Never!!"

"And what is this card you speak of?"

"Oh, if you are a professional, such as a lawyer or a nurse or doctor you have a business card with your name, title, cell phone and maybe work number. You can give these out to others, not just men, so they may contact you again if they wish."

It takes quite awhile to explain her job, her condo, living alone, and how she gets around but finally she has a chance to ask if life is any better for these women.

Labiba speaks up, "You must know that for us, for me, this is the only time I can be myself! I can not in my own home when my husband or his family is around. I must be what do you say? Oh *yes, submissive (in English)* but here tonight we talk about anything we want, we feel safe."

Jada jumps in, "But it was better before, before you know, the American invasion. Now the men have become cowards with the Mullahs all going on about what the Koran says we must do, how we must be submissive, it is, how you say, *stupid !* Many women have been beaten by the "beards" even in the streets but many also at home.

Atiyah knows that the "Beards" is a negative for men who have now adopted the old ways and think they know what is right and proper and try to force others to do the same.

Jada goes on, "The men have submitted to the mullahs and then they bring these crazy ideas home. We wanted to believe things would get better with so called democracy but it is not so for most of us."

Jada with a stern look asks, "Atiyah, what of this American infidel we have heard about? What has happened with him? You have seem him?"

Atiyah studies Jada's face to see where this is going but can not quite tell. "Jada, I have not seen him.I do no know what he is doing or where he is. I do miss him. You may not approve or understand but he is a good man." The ladies make high keening noises and roll their eyes and there is some "Atiyah, this is not good, tsk,tsk." but then the matter is dropped.

As the night goes on the women play loud Persian music and show off their dancing skills. Atiyah is pulled to her feet and encouraged to join, though she protests she has forgotten so much. In the end they are all dancing and laughing and seem like old friends.

Finally Atiyah, the girls, and Shilan take their leave and head home. Few people are on the streets and even fewer women, but they don't have far to go and soon are home. Atiyah let's Shilan know how much fun she has had and thanks Shilan profusely.

CHAPTER TWENTY ONE

10:24 AM, November 15, 2011

Jamilla, Iraq

Later that week Atiyah and Shilan, with the girls in tow, were headed to the local bazaar to purchase food for the day. Most days Shilan had to go out and buy food since she could not depend on the small refrigerator to keep foods very long after the electricity went out, which was almost every afternoon. As they turned a corner and pushed their way through the crowded street filled with cars, goats, carts, and donkeys a young man, tall and solidly built, dressed in camouflage pants and a shabby military green coat approached with head down as if he didn't see them coming. They stopped in their tracks to wait for him to pass but he did not, he abruptly stopped and stared at Atiyah, "My sister, may Allah bless you, do you not know your own brother??"

"Oh, oh, this can not be!!" Atiyah shrieked and put her hands in the air with excitement! Shilan and the girls joined in wailing and bending before Siamak.

Grabbing Siamak's hands Atiyah exclaims, "My dear brother Siamak! You are alive and well?? Where have you been and how are you?" Where do you live? Oh, dear Siamak, I am prattling like a child but this is so unexpected!! Please come join us for tea, we must talk!!"

"Yes, I can do that, if you will. Let's continue on to the shop around the corner. Hello my dear cousins, may Allah shine his blessing on you!"

The girls bowed and lowered their eyes not daring to speak to their cousin, whom they knew very little of.

Arriving at the small cafe they ordered tea and soft drinks for the girls. Oh, Siamak you are thin but you look good. I was so afraid for you. I do not wish to know what happened to you in prison but you survived and now you are here!"

They paused and waited for the young man to pour the tea, leave small cookies and soft drinks for the girls and they all said, "Shukran."

"Yes, but I am here to confront you, dear sister. Your past contacts with this American Jew brought the will of Allah down upon your head and if the marines had not found us the Jew would be dead. You made a grave error in being with him. You know the Qur'an does not allow for this mingling of devout Muslims and infidels! Yet you persisted. I learned only a short while ago that our dear father died in the land of the infidels and now you are back here for what purpose?"

"Dear brother I must tell you I may not believe as you do or at least in the way you do. We have grown in different directions since we were young. I am not a slave to the belief's of my childhood. I would hope you have learned to be merciful and understand Allah does not want us to treat one another with hatred and judgement, that we may find peace in our lives and kindness toward one another. Do not judge me, as surely Allah has not set aside this power for you alone, and if we all rush to judge, the world will only continue to fester with hatred and killing. Seek a peaceful heart dear brother. I will be here only another week or so and will then return to my home and job in the states."

"I will find peace when I have the Jew by the throat once again and if you stay you may have to pay retribution for your sins also. You have dishonored the Rashid name and brought shame upon our family."

"You are not the patriarch of the family, he is dead, may Allah bless him. Do not threaten me. I am not a coward who like most women here, run from you, or any man. I will not accept this from you my brother, or any man. I wish you well and it brings me joy to know you are well. Please let us part with gentle words and ask Allah to bless each of us. I do not want any more of these harsh words in front of our sweet cousins. Now if you can not accept me as your sister who loves you, please go in peace."

"I came here to ask you to renounce your past and to assure me you will now follow the path Allah has provided. I see this is not in your heart and now tell you that you must go or face the consequences of your sins. When we meet next it will not be with joy. Alaikum assalam."

With this he rose, threw money on the table and quickly turned his back on them leaving Atiyah, Shilan and the girls sitting alone shaking and confused as to what was next. Atiyah was saddened by her brothers response, hoping that time had softened his heart, but it was clear this was not to be. She was proud of herself for standing up to him but she also now realized she had endangered her cousin and she could not stay long in her house.

CHAPTER TWENTY TWO

12:57 PM, November 17, 2011

Jamilla, Iraq

Atiyah and her cousin had been out walking the bazaars and shopping for groceries. Atiyah spent long hours talking to Shilan and her girls about her life in the states. The girls giggled and stared in rapt attention to hear about her life. They did watch television and they knew what America looked like, or what they believed it looked like, but hearing Atiyah talk about her city where colorful trains ran on cables buried in the streets, huge bodies of water where huge ships from all over the world traveled under big bridges painted red, and women dressed in fancy clothes walking alone in the city. They couldn't believe her stories.

Shilan finally spoke about the meeting with Siamak, wringing her hands as she walked, "Dear Atiyah, what will you do now? I fear for your life! I know these men and they have become very dangerous and I also see that Siamak has become one of them. They will force or convince him to do something, and it will all be done in the name of Allah. Please do not take his words lightly!"

"Yes, and I do not want to bring trouble down on your home dear Shilan. I do not believe Siamak will act right away. His threats are to scare me and he would hope that I will come to him and ask for forgiveness. This I can not and will not do. I know longer believe as he does and especially that a man can use Allah's name to try and intimidate a woman. But I'm afraid my visit will have to be much shorter than I might want." Atiyah reaches out and hugs Shilan. "Please if you can, allow me a few more days here and then I will be on my way home."

"There is no problem unless my husband finds out about Siamak coming to visit, then I am sure he will demand you leave our home." Shilan pushes back and her face conveys deep concern.

Late in the night, Atiyah alone in the main room on her rug with pillows around her and only a little light from around the drapes on the windows leaking into the dark, thought of how she felt about being back here. Her life had changed so much for the better, and how her cousins life had changed so much for the worse. What a contrast now, and as much as she would like to help her cousin it was clear Shilan would not hear of it.

Thoughts of her family, her brother Siamak, and David also pushed into her conscience. "*What was Siamak up to? Was he serious about his threats to her? She loved her brother but to listen to him speak as he did it was a voice she did not know. How had he allowed these people to poison his mind and now would make threats to kill his sister? Was David involved as a possible target again? Was he even here in Baghdad?*" Finally sleep crept upon her and the worries of the day slipped away.

CHAPTER TWENTY THREE

9:12 AM, November 18, 2011

Baghdad, Iraq

David is visiting the clinic again, supervising installation of medical equipment when his cell phone goes off. He checks the screen and sees it's his buddy Paul Burkhart. He decides to take the call and steps outside for privacy.

"Hey Paul! What's up?"

"David, thought I'd get back to you with what I've learned about your little Princess. Yeah, I've learned quite a bit about her. First, you might want to sit down!"

Davids heart beat notched up a couple of clicks. Oh shit! This can't be good!"

"Well, that all depends I guess. From my point of view, it's not, but maybe from yours it is. She's alive and has been living in San Francisco since the U.S. embassy arranged for her and her father to leave the country after the kidnapping was aborted. Her old man died a couple of years ago. She is a nurse at UCSF Medical Center. Now the best part! Ready?"

"Yeah, I guess! Give it to me!"

"She's here in Baghdad!"

His heart was already racing when he heard this but now he was shaking as he responded. "What! You gotta be kiddin'?"

"No my friend I kid not! She's reported visiting her cousin in Jamilla. Do you know the area?"

"Wow! Damn! Yeah, that's where her family lived when I was helping them reconstruct their business. This is hard to believe. All these years I was afraid she was dead and she's been living in San Francisco! If only I had known!"

"Yeah, if only you had known you would have been hated by the father, I'm sure of that! Now buddy, I'm telling you to stay away from this hornet's nest! If you are seen with this woman by any of her family you put yourself, and her in grave danger. These people, as you well know, do not put up with their women seeing infidels and strolling around in broad daylight. I can't protect you from what might happen again! Tell me you will not act on what I've just told you! She is supposed to be here for a short time hoping to bring her cousin back with her to the states. My source at the embassy says that will not happen so she may not stay here very long."

"Damn Paul, I can't tell you what I'll do right now. This is so startling I need some time to think about it. I hear you and I know this could be, no, is very dangerous for me, and Atiyah also. Thanks for getting back to me. Talk later OK?"

Yeah, but don't do anything stupid over a women, especially this woman! Bye."

Feeling light headed David mumbles "Bye" folds his phone and stares at it as if a strange alien object.

David stood there in the bight sunlight thinking about what he had just been told. *"She's alive! She's here in Jamilla! She's been in San Francisco for years and I didn't know! What the Hell! Now what? I want to see her but shit !Paul is right! This is dangerous and I don't want any part of what happened last time. Shit! Shit! Shit! ... gotta be careful."*

Paul had provided the address in Jamilla where Atiyah's cousin lived. David knew he had to at least make contact with the cousin or if possible Atiyah and let her know he was here in the city.

Quickly stabbing Jamal's number into his phone, "Jamal, please pick me up at my place in an hour. Yes, it will be a visit to a home in Jamilla and should not take more than an hour of your time. OK, see you soon."

Jamal honked outside and David picked up his phone, keys and closed the apt door feeling the bright desert sun, but also today noticing the coolness of the morning air. The first signs of fall were here and it was a relief from the insufferable heat of summer. He looked both ways as he descended the stairs to Jamal and his awaiting car.

Jamal greeted David, "Good morning David and where are we off to this fine morning?"

"Jamal your English is getting to be very good, you know! I must see a friend in Jamilla and I will need to ask if you will go to the door and ask for her. She is a guest in her cousins house and it would be better to have you go to the door, than a foreigner." He gives Jamal a questioning look, "Are you OK doing this?"

"No prob bro! Give me address and let's, how you say? Vamoose!!"

It always amazed David how Iraqis' picked up slang so fast from Western TV shows. Jamal was a religious man but not a zealot and he was fascinated by Western ways. He and his family watched Western shows on the few channels that were available via satellite dish.

Jamal found the address and David recognized it as just around the corner from where the Rashid family had lived. Jamal stopped the car, turned and looking in the car mirrors for any trouble asked David, "What is her name please?"

David told him, "Ask for Atiyah. If Atiyah comes to the door, ask her to meet a man named David at the cafe where they used to go for tea."

Jamal took this in with suspicious eyes cast at David but said nothing. David watched closely as Jamal went to the door. He watched the street also for any trouble. Jamal knocked and David saw a woman come to the door with eyes downcast and heard Jamal pass on the information. The woman put her hand to her lips and her eyes turned to the car. She said something to Jamal and then closed the door. Jamal turned and motioned to David with one finger indicating he was to wait.

Suddenly the door opened, Atiyah rushed out, saw the car and looked in and saw David. She hushed a scream with a hand to her mouth and with a smile that lit up her face she ran to the car, opened the door, and reaching in hugged David.

"Oh, my dear David! You are alive!! I can't believe this! Can I ..."

With a warm smile and eyes glued to hers, David pushed her back but held her saying, "Dear Atiyah it's wonderful to see you again but we must be careful. Please, as hard as it may be, go in now and arrange to meet me at the cafe where we used to go. You know which one? "

"Yes, of course. When?"

"Tomorrow at 3 would be great if you can?"

"I will David. Should I come alone?"

"It would be better if your cousin came along but I'll let you make that decision. Now you should go back in."

Atiyah looked up and down the street and seeing no one turned and kissed David quickly. David kissed her back and then pulled away saying, "I'll see you at 3 tomorrow. Bye my love. Go now and be safe."

"Oh, David this is so wonderful. I have dreamed of you so often and hoped and prayed you were alright. I'll be there at 3. Bye for now"

Atiyah entered her cousins house floating on air, unable to talk, almost sobbing, she was so excited.

Her cousin pestered her immediately asking,

"Atiyah! Atiyah! Who was that man? Was that this David soldier you were with before the incident? She never said "kidnapping" as if that sounded too sinful a thing for a good Muslim to do to anyone. Please tell me?"

Atiyah was grateful that Shilan's husband was not here, he would not have approved and might have passed on the fact that there was a strange man at his house to elders in the community who had contacts with insurgents.

"Shilan it would be best if you not know anything about this and I will be going out later tomorrow alone. I ask that you keep this to yourself or say only that I have gone to see some people I knew from the states. I can not risk bringing trouble to you and your girls."

"Atiyah, I am your dear cousin and friend and I"ll swear to Allah this shall be between us. I know you will be careful and you know well what your brother Siamak has said and you must be careful he may have someone watching even now."

"I know and I am worried for all of us. I will see what David's plans are and make decisions that will keep us safe. She takes Shilan's hands in hers. Please do not worry Shilan, I'll not let this come back on you."

"Atiyah, in the name of Allah please be careful and know I want you to be safe. You should not be out alone on the streets, let me go with you?"

"No, this I can not do, Shilan. Please, you go shopping as you normally would, do not do anything that is different from what you do. I will go out tomorrow for a short visit at the bazaar. I will let you know my plans after that when I come back."

Meanwhile, Taariq sees her from an abandoned house just down the street from Shilan's. He sees the car pull up and unfold the Rashid woman rushing out to the car. He can not be sure who is in the car but he suspects it is the American. His eyes narrow with hatred and suspicion of what his sister is up to.

Using his cell phone he greets Siamak with derision dripping from his voice, "Alaikum assalam, Siamak! Your beloved sister has met with someone in a car that pulled up to the house. I can only assume it is the target in the car!"

"Alaikum assalam, it is not a good time to act and I do not want to involve anyone who may be innocent. Please we must be off the phone. I have the resources for our event. Continue your mission. Call me with further details."

'As you wish."

Siamak was in a different house. If they were being followed or phone traced they would not all be in one place. He took time to again say his prayers and ask Allah for a sign as to what he should do. He went through the vest, the electronics hooked to it, the pistol and the ammo, all was in order. He had been trained how to assemble the vest and how to detonate it with the cell phone or just a sudden impact. He did not want to die but we all must and if he could take out some infidels and be promised a place in heaven it seemed a good bargain and with the added benefit of restoring his family's honor. Now he would wait for word from Taariq and Faaris, then meet close to wherever his sister was, intercept her, pull her into the car, strap the vest on her and proceed to the checkpoint where she would be thrown out. When she pleaded for help from the U.S. soldiers they would see her vest, shoot her and the vest would be detonated. Hopefully, bringing death to many of the infidels and his dear sister who had lost her way.

CHAPTER TWENTY FOUR

10:12 AM, November 19, 2011

Baghdad, Iraq

David's cell rang, "David, good morning. There are some developments you need to be made aware of. I have someone passing on intel concerning your sister. And since you didn't listen to my warning, I'm telling you again you are putting yourself and this women in grave danger."

His shoulders sag as he hers Paul's words, "Paul what's going on?"

"She is also being watched by other eyes. These eyes belong to a small Al Qaeda cell, which includes your girlfriend's brother Siamak! Again! I don't have complete details but what we have indicates something is going down in the next couple of days. If you have plans to see her again I am warning you for the last time, stay away form her!"

After the phone call, David sat there staring out the window considering his moves. Fear is creeping into his blood. Should he try to see Atiyah and warn her? Should he go to her cousin's house or wait until they meet at the bazaar? It seemed neither was a good choice, but leaving her vulnerable didn't seem like something he could do either. He decided the best bet was to go to the bazaar and find a secluded place where they would not be seen. When Atiyah showed up he would have Jamal drop a note to her warning her she was being watched and telling her his plans.

He had decided that there was only one way for them to ever have a life together and that was to meet again somewhere that was safe. He had purchased two one way flights out of Baghdad for two days from now with a stop over in Istanbul. She would have to decide if she wanted to go with him or not but they could not stay here, that was certain.

That same day Atiyah was nervous but fully committed to meeting David. She was going to tell him, as much as she wanted to see him she could not do that here in Baghdad under these circumstances. She would ask him if he was willing to give up his job here and come back to the States. She would go where ever he wanted. They could have a normal life together but it could not be here and not now. She told her cousin Shilan it would be only a few days and she would return to the States.

She picked up her day pack, covered her head with one of her cousins black burghas and headed out the door. She wore the burgha, which she hated as a symbol of the domination of Muslim women but now wore as a mask to hide behind. Hoping no one would notice her, she walked the few blocks to the bazaar. Entering the main street she stood, looked around, and seeing nothing suspicious, only a few other women, heads down, burgha or hajib covering their faces as they carried their bags, she walked quickly to the bazaar. Cars covered in street dust bumped and rattled down the street weaving around people and pot holes caused by bombs or IEDs. She kept her eyes down, but scanned the streets for trouble, knowing that even on the best days she was in some danger out here.

Paul and his assistant Joe were parked on the side of the street and had been for several hours, watching the Rashid house. They had seen a man come out and assumed he was the cousins husband. Now they saw a woman come out, dressed in a black burgha, looking around as she entered the street then moving quickly down the street away from them. They had no clear way to know this was Atiyah but she was of slender build, obvious even in the Muslim dress. They had seen Atiyah and her cousin days before and noted the cousin was heavier and bulkier. From this they felt sure this was Atiyah and Paul's skin crawled knowing she was vulnerable now, a fragile black moth flitting down a dusty sun filled street for an encounter with the darkness of death. He didn't know where or exactly when but this was a perfect opportunity for Al Qaeda to strike.

Atiyah was only two blocks from her cousin's house when she noticed a beat up old car approaching. It was a brown Mercedes with spider cracks in the windshield and the windows were so dirty she could not see occupants but thought there were two men in the car. None of this was very different from most of the other cars on the street but she was hypersensitive and something about the way it moved slowly towards her scared her and made the hair on her arms stand up. She stopped walking and waited for it to go by. Just as it pulled even with her she recognized Siamak as the driver, turned to run but the door on her side flew open, a man jumped out and grabbed her by the arm, threw her roughly into the back seat and threw himself on top of her. She tried to scream but quickly her captor placed a hand over her mouth, so hard she bit her tongue and tasted blood. Within a few seconds he pushed his knees into her back and wrapped what she assume was duct tape across her mouth, followed by tape around her hands, which had been yanked behind her back. He then moved on to her ankles and pulled her ankles to her back behind her knees wrapping her ankles to her legs with the tape. She was trussed and bound like the goat herders do when bringing goats to market. She attempted to scream at Siamak but could barely breathe. She could hear him as he partly turned towards the back seat.

With a calm sneering smile he says, "Dear Atiyah, I was gracious and kind and warned you of your sins and that any further sinning with this infidel would cause you great harm. You did not heed my warning and now I must, in the name of Allah, restore honor to the Rashid name. You may have noticed I am a little fatter now! Yes, I have put on some weight, in fact I have about 20 kilos of explosives and shrapnel in the vest I am wearing. I will share this gift now with these infidels at the checkpoint ahead and then you will be the second surprise! I have no fear now my dear sister and so you should also have no fear, as I am taking you with me to sit before Allah. He will bring his judgement on us for eternity and I have a clear conscience. I am not so sure for you but I hope you will ask for his mercy and forgiveness." Atiyah continues to struggle and mumbles words that are lost to her captors.

Siamak pulled over on the side of the road and reached down below the passenger seat and picked up a vest from the floor. It was quite heavy and required some effort as he pulled it up over the seat and handed it to Taariq.

"Here is the vest for her. Place it on her as best you can."

Paul follows, just far enough back to see what they are up to, knowing he could be spotted at any moment and Siamak could do something stupid.

Siamak waited a few minutes noticing that there were no pedestrians close by while Taariq wrestled with the vest, pushing and prodding it around Atiyah's slender shoulders and over her breasts where he tied it with the built in cords. There were pockets sewn inside the vest where the packets of explosives were inserted and wired one to the other. On the outside were pockets where nails and ball bearings were inserted as killing projectiles when the vest blew up. It was heavy and cumbersome but Tariq now had it in place around Atiyah's upper body making her appear as some kind of rag doll.

Atiyah's eyes filled with tears, she glared at her captors, struggling uselessly as a wild trapped animal might, but it was of no use struggling against the restraints. Terror soon took the place of tears as she realized what her brother was going to do.

Raising his voice in a mocking tone Siamak said, "Yes, dear sister, you seem to have guessed right! We will go one after the other and take out as many of these infidels as possible. The checkpoint is only a couple of miles from here. It should not be long and we will both be free. And for you it is a special vest! No detonator needed! You see, when we release you and put you out on the street the soldiers will see you have a vest and they will come to shoot you. After you have been released on the street I will ram the car into the checkpoint which will detonate my explosives and take out quite a few infidels, they will expect a second attack and when they see you they will shoot you. Of course my dear sister, Allah will be merciful and you will die from either a bullet or from the explosion from your vest. Simple? Yes? I suggest you walk straight towards the checkpoint so they don't shoot you in the back. No one will offer to help you as they will see the vest and run for their lives. Only a soldier will stop you and that will be with a bullet which will set off the explosives. Trust me you will feel nothing! And I'll go first and show you the way to heaven!"

With that Siamak stopped the car, looked at Taariq and said, "Alaikum assalam! Now go with her, wait in the alley and release her as soon as you know I have done my duty. May Allah have mercy on you Atiyah."

Taariq looked at Siamak with knowing eyes, got out, cut the tape from Atiyah's legs, ripped it from her mouth and pulled her with him, as he dragged her around the corner into an alley.

Siamak with tears in his eyes speaks to her, saying again, "May Allah have mercy on you, my dear sister."

Paul and his aide Allen watched and as soon as they saw Taariq pull Atiyah, struggling, from the car they sped up, approaching the vehicle quickly. They could hear Atiyah screaming for help, screaming for Siamak not to do this, and waving her arms desperately.

Paul driving, turned to Allen, "You have your ID band on your arm? Good, we don't want those soldiers to fire on us! I'm calling the Spec Ops now to alert them to our position. Also, I'll turn the cell phone blocker on so you should be safe from the vest if they are using a cell detonator!"

Paul saw what was going down in a second and told Allen, "Get the driver! Now! Don't miss or those guys in the checkpoint are toast! When you see that guy who grabbed Atiyah come back out to see what happened, nail him!!

With one swift movement Allen raised his rifle, sighted and fired at the driver of the car ahead. A huge explosion blew up in front of them where the vehicle had been moments before! Car parts flew, whistled by, and landed everywhere, hitting their vehicle and ricocheting off houses, walls on each side of the street, and smoke immediately filled the air, along with acrid smells of burning debris and human flesh.

Allen turned in the seat, opened the passenger door, saw the guy come out to see what had happened, with a strong grip on Atiyah's arm. Allen had only a moment to make the shot. Bam, bam!! The guy dropped like a rock, flat on the sidewalk and Atiyah screamed, thinking she was next.

Blood sprayed on Atiyah, her face, her clothes, Taariq had ripped the tape off her mouth and now she screamed as bits of rock and plaster hit her face and dug into her skin. She staggered around the body and fell screaming to her knees.

Paul yelled to Atiyah, "You are safe, go back around the corner and Allen here will take the vest off you! Don't run or the soldiers will shoot you!"

Atiyah was petrified but heard Paul and turned staggering back around the corner. People were already on the street and saw her and instantly knew from experience that she had a suicide vest. Allen got out and slowly approached Atiyah. He raised his arm displaying the ID Band to the soldiers.

He shouted to Atiyah, "Ok, little lady do you know if you are wearing a detonator? Did they say how they would blow up the explosives?"

Screaming, "Oh God please! I don't really know! They said I would blow up when the soldiers shot me! I don't think they used a detonator. Please help me before the soldiers get here and shoot me! I don't want to die! Not now!"

With that Allen saw a soldier approach with rifle at the ready. "Don't shoot! I'm going to her! There is no detonator but I'm going to approach slowly and check her out. Cover me!"

With this, he walked slowly, talking to Atiyah as he did. "Did you see a little black box with wires hanging from it anywhere on that vest?"

Still screaming "No!No! But I was so scared and they threw me on the seat and tied me before putting the vest on me! Please get me out of this!"

"Did you feel that guy reach over and click a little box or hear him say he had activated the device?"

Falling to her knees, "No, My brother Siamak said they would shoot me and that would be it!"

Now Allen used his hands in a calming motion as he talked Atiyah into calming down, "Lady! Easy now,I think we're OK. I'm going to slowly look around on the vest and then I'll place my hands on the edges and feel carefully. Are you OK with this?"

Her voice trembled, her body shook as she said, "Yes,yes, please be careful. I am so scared! "

Allen moved his hand carefully around the vest, feeling for wires. He found none. "OK, next we're going to slowly cut these cords that hold the vest on. We're going to go slow just in case I missed something." He cut one at a time, and after each he looked at her and asked, "OK?" Atiyah continued to tremble and would nod and he would move to the next one. Sweat was pouring from his face but he ignored it and worked slowly and meticulously until all the cords were cut. Atiyah slumped in his arms as he cut the last cord.

He called to the soldier who was still standing there at a safe distance around the corner. "Hey buddy!! Come here and give me a hand!"

The soldier peered around the corner and Allen motioned for him to come over. He ran up, stopped and approached slowly seeing the vest.

"OK, we're going to slowly lift this thing off her. I'm pretty sure it's safe but it's still a lot of shit and I don't want to do anything stupid now!" They grabbed the vest and carefully lifted and Atiyah moaned, shivered and cried, "Oh, please. please let me live!"

Allen nodded to the soldier, "Take it around the corner", as the vest came off Atiyah. Allen, holding Atiyah by her shoulders, walks Atiyah over to the curb where they see Paul and other soldiers inspecting the crater where the car had been. Allen yelled to Paul, "Looks like we need bomb squad here Paul!"

"OK, I've already called them, they should be here any minute or hour! You know how that goes!" Allen and Atiyah walked over and Atiyah gasped as she saw the crater and then wailed, "Oh Siamak! Why? What good did this do? My dear brother, you are all I had left!" She sank to her knees sobbing, "What has happened to my country? All we do is kill each other! When will this stop??"

He told Allen to give Atiyah a lift back to her cousins house and with that Atiyah followed Allen to the car.

Paul stayed behind to explain to the police how they knew what Siamak was up to. He stays to answer questions about what happened. This was outside his security job but he had authority to deal with issues like this when he came upon them. He would have to fill out a report but that would most likely be the extent of his involvement.

Atiyah was still shaking and sobbing when she entered the house. Shilan seeing Atiyah at the door sobbing, with her clothes ripped and dirty asked, "Oh My God, what happened?"

"Siamak tried to kill me in a suicide attack. Oh, God, it was so horrible!" as she slumped down on the couch trying to catch her breath.

"Where is Siamak now?"

"He is dead. He blew himself up! He's with Allah now, I guess! How could he do this? He was followed by someone, no, two men. I don't know how but they are involved with David. They saw him ready to drive into the checkpoint and shot him before he could get there. His vest, the car, his body all gone! Nothing left but pieces! Siamak had someone with him who grabbed me, threw me in the car, put a suicide vest on me, then dragged me out of the car and was going to push me out in the street where the soldiers would see me and shoot me! One of the men who followed Siamak, shot the man who was holding me then came over and helped get the vest off me! If it wasn't for him I would be dead! Splattered all over the street like Siamak! What is wrong with us? Why do we do these horrible things and claim Allah wants us to kill like this??

Shilan held Atiyah, comforting her and sobbing at the same time. They stayed like this for awhile as the girls came out of the back room and stared at them, asking what was wrong?

"Darlings, nothing is wrong now. Some men tried to scare Atiyah but she is brave and she is fine now. Go play." And off they went to play with their dolls, no idea of the tragedy that had just unfolded.

CHAPTER TWENTY FIVE

1:35 PM, November 19, 2011

Jamilla, Baghdad

Atiyah rested and tried to eat some lunch to no avail, then called the cell phone number David had provided. He answered with, "Are you OK? I heard from Paul what happened! My God that was close! You must be terrified! You can not stay here any longer Atiyah, nor can I. We are targets for sure. The other members of this cell will seek revenge. We must go!"

"Yes, I understand and I am terrified now of what they may still do to me! But how is it, again I must leave because of mad men who wish to kill me? What have I done that brings on this madness?? What do you want to do? You have your job here? What will you do?"

"Atiyah, I have already made plans. We must go to Istanbul as soon as possible. I have tickets for a flight out tonight at 11 PM. I will be there waiting for you. Do not show up until 30 minutes before the flight as you may be followed and hanging around the gate may give someone a chance to harm you. I have talked to my boss and he understands I must leave, at least for now. We should not stay on the phone as your phone may be bugged. Are you OK with these plans?"

"Yes, I don't have much choice. I'll pack my things and find a driver to take me somewhere to wait until it is time to meet you. Poor Shilan, I hate leaving her and the girls but she says she will not go."

"Atiyah, I'll send Jamal to pick you up. He can be trusted and knows places to go and wait that will be safe. You must pack and be ready to meet him within the hour. Understood?"

"Yes, I'll look for him outside. Thank you David."

"OK, I have told him to go and get you. Watch for the car and get in quickly. Be very careful my dear, do not stop anywhere, let him take you to a safe place. I'll see you tonight at the airport."

Atiyah hung up staring at her phone and thought, *"I hope they weren't listening in!"* She quickly washed herself and changed to clean clothes. She packed while again telling Shilan how sorry she was for bringing this trouble to her door.

Shilan reassured her it was not her fault. She said, "My country is now going mad! These men are sick with paranoia and loss of what is good and fair. They no longer know who they are and seek power and control of women to give their lives meaning. Allah did not do this, they have done it themselves. My girls will be educated and Allah willing they may find a better life!"

"Shilan, I promise I will do what I can to help you and the girls. Anytime you want me to I will work to get visas for you and them."

"Not for me, but when they are a little older I will ask if you can get them out of here and into a good university like where you studied."

She turned and hugged Shilan, "I promise I will do that for you and for them."

She had gathered all her things and now waited for Jamal to pull to a stop. She was in the courtyard with Shilan and the girls, they could still hear sirens from up the street where the bomb had gone off. Atiyah was still shaking when she thought back on what took place. The air had a smell of burned chemicals that still hung in the air to remind her of the horror. She could still recall the whumph! Of air being pushed down the street as if some huge hand had slammed down on the street and around the corner and then the terrible baroom! of explosives, metal, plastic, dirt, stones, pieces of asphalt, all raining down on the street, careening against buildings, pinging off cars. The man who held her yanking her into the street and the sudden smacking sound as a bullet blew a hole in his head and a red mist of blood covered her head and chest. He was dropped like a bag of potatoes! One second he was there in front of her and the next he was on the sidewalk, dead, a large hole in what had been his head now oozing blood onto the street. After that it was all a blur. The man, his name was Allen, had shot the bad guy, and called for help to remove the vest. It was all a blur and really, that is where she wanted to keep it. She did not want the details now and probably never would.

CHAPTER TWENTY SIX

7:23 PM, November 19, 2011

Jamilla, Baghdad

She heard the car horn and looked through the gate and saw Jamal was there looking anxiously for her. She kissed and hugged Shilan and the girls and hurried out to the car. Jamal greeted her, "Alaikum assalam, and I am sorry for what has taken place. We must leave here immediately, please get down in the rear so you will not be seen."

She did as requested and Jamal tore through the streets, careening around corners and stopping every couple of blocks to check if they were being followed. This went on for at least an hour, he pulled up to a gate jumped out after looking around, opened the gate, drove the car through and closed the gate. He motioned to Atiyah to come out and she followed him inside. The house was clean and neat but with very little furniture. Jamal showed her the kitchen and bathroom. He told her she would be safe here. He would wait with her until it was time to go to the airport. He offered her tea and some biscuits which she was happy to have since she had eaten very little. They talked a little about what happened and Atiyah's hands still shook with fear, Jamal was reticent to share his life and shy with her. He asked if she needed something to read but she demurred since she had a book to read then went into a small adjacent room and said he would be napping and please knock if she needed anything. She sat and thought about all that had happened and now could only hope that David would meet her and they could fly out here safely.

A few hours later, in the middle of the night, Jamal came out of the room, used the bathroom and when he came out told her to get ready to leave for the airport. Atiyah was nervous and still shook with fear when she thought of what had taken place only hours before. She used the shower and quickly changed clothes for the flight to Istanbul only a couple of hours away now. It was dark and Jamal did the same crazy driving pattern and it pleased Atiyah to know he was doing his best to protect her, even if it was at the instructions of his boss, David. Arriving at the airport, they had to go through a checkpoint and Atiyah had to show her visa and tickets. Jamal dropped her at the departure gate and told her to wait inside, David would find her and not to worry. He politely bade her good bye and when she tried to tip him he declined repeatedly until she gave up. She entered the gray concrete nondescript building, and hurried through security with no problem. She had about an hour before the flight and was very anxious to leave this crazy place. Twenty minutes later David walked through security and hurried up to her. They hugged for a long time but gave no other indications of intimacy.

"Atiyah! My darling! I was so worried! Are you sure you're OK? Did Jamal treat you well?"

"Yes, yes, he was very good and gracious! Please treat him well!" It took some time before Atiyah could pull herself away from David's embrace.

`They moved on to their gate and had only about 30 minutes to wait for their flight to be called. Soon they were side by side watching the arid desert slide by below the wings of the jet, silver and gold in the light cast by the moon. After a couple of hours they could see the dark blue of the Black Sea as they turned eastward to Istanbul, Turkey. Atiyah found herself dozing off, resting her head on David's shoulder, as events of the day caught up with her.

David already enjoyed having this woman in his life again but now a future together was real and led to all kinds of thoughts, hopes and decisions to be made. He had collected few possessions in Iraq and the few that he could not bring with him, Jamal would ship to him when he had an address. It seemed practical for him to move to San Francisco, since he had no other place that he really called home. Would Atiyah be OK with this? Would she want him to get his own place for awhile? So much to think about but now they had time and would be safe in Istanbul.

CHAPTER TWENTY SEVEN

11:30 PM, November 20, 2011

Istanbul, Turkey

"May I have your attention. In preparation for landing please reset your seats to their full upright position and store any objects you may have taken out during the flight. Thank you, we will be landing shortly."

The city twinkled in the last dark of night and lights reflected on the water along the bay front.

They found a cab, the hotel, which was the same one they had stayed at previously and the same one Atiyah had stayed at when she had come to Baghdad less than a month ago. They enjoyed the old byzantine look of the furniture, tapestries, and architecture in the old but comfortable place.

David opened the door to their room, turned on a light and put his bags down on the bed. Atiyah followed doing the same and then turned to David. They stood for a second, Atiyah's eyes wet, still fearful, eyes filled with questions. David broke the silence, "Atiyah it is so good to see you and know I can kiss you or give you a hug but I know you have gone through a terrible experience today and don't want to push too hard with intimacy you may not be able to handle?"

Atiyah moved up to him looking him straight in the eye and said, "David, shut up, hold me and kiss me!"

And so they fell upon one another kissing, hugging and falling together on the bed. After some hugging, kissing and fondling Atiyah said, "OK buddy, I think I need a shower after today's fall out! I feel like my hair is covered with bomb dust, shrapnel and God knows what else! It's a wonder my clothes didn't set off the bomb detector at airport security!"

She pulled clothes and her toiletry bag out of her suitcase and went off to the shower. She was back in a moment telling David, "I love this old place, the bath is so over the top with opulence it makes me feel like a princess!"

"My sweet heart, you are a princess!"

"Oh, David you are my prince! I'll be out in a few minutes." The shower was running and David stayed on his back on the bed trying to sort out all that had happened. Paul had left an email for him indicating that all was settled, the police accepted his version that he had been following Siamak and Taariq for a few miles based on intel he had. He told the police he had no definite knowledge of a time and place for this incident, and as they were following they saw what went down and were forced to intervene when Atiyah was kidnapped and it was clear Siamak and Taariq were going to blow up the checkpoint.

The Iraqi police had not been happy they were contacted after the fact but what could they do? Paul's last words to David were, "Have a great time in Istanbul and don't come back!" David couldn't agree more but knew he would miss his people working in the clinics. He had left a lot of his things in Baghdad to Jamal and also gave him a nice bit of cash to help him out until he could get another job.

Atiyah let the hot water run and soak away the sorrow and pain and finally felt good about joining David. The door to the bathroom opened and Atiyah stepped out wearing a short little nightie, and he exclaimed, "Whoa! Now that doesn't meet dress code in Baghdad! Where did you come up with that?"

"Shut up! You're embarrassing me! When I was shopping here waiting for my plane to Baghdad I found this lingerie shop and I thought what if I do find David? What would I wear and this just popped into my hand! You like it?"

"Do I like it! Well come here and let me check it out!"

Atiyah moved over to the bed and sat down next to David and David slid his hand along her leg, softly moving up her thigh pushing the light black lingerie aside as he went higher and higher.

David heard Atiyah catch her breath and then said, "OK, I better go take a shower too! I'm pretty grungy and I need to clean up. Be right out! Don't go anywhere! Well, not dressed like that anyway!"

Atiyah reached for Davids hand and placed it on her breast and said in a sexy breathy voice, "Don't hurry, take your time!"

David came out of the shower with the towel wrapped around his waist, came to the bed next to Atiyah and said, "Do I need to change?"

Atiyah looked up with a sexy grin, "Give me that towel you silly man!"

She grabbed the towel from his waist and pulled him down on the bed next to her. They kissed slowly and softly, acknowledging it had been a long time but felt so good to be together again. Soon the lingerie was off and David was softly exploring Atiyah's body, lightly stroking her nipples, brushing his fingers down her stomach and kissing her as he move lower. Atiyah's little gasps of excitement told him he was welcome to keep going and he did. He found her wet and excited and he found himself hard. They moved so each could please the other and Atiyah softly said. "You know how difficult this was for me at first?"

"Yes, I remember." As he nuzzled her ear.

"Now it seems so right and I look forward to pleasing you and having you do the same for me. I've changed so much and so much for the better. Thank you David!" And with that took him into her mouth and he licked her with his tongue. They made love slowly, until Atiyah could no longer take it and told David she needed him in her now! They inhaled each other, entwined themselves in each other, and finally climaxed with sweat pouring off their skin, laying next to each other softly holding hands. Feeling their heart beats slow down and the air from the slowly turning overhead fans caressing them.

In the deep of the night Atiyah awoke screaming, "No! No! Siamak! Don't ..." David sat up and hugged her, "It's OK, I'm here, it's OK. It's over my dear Atiyah." She then knew where she was and took a deep breath, snuggled against him letting warm tears fall.

Morning found them at a small cafe enjoying coffee and pastries, close to the Grand Bazaar. The weather in Istanbul, in the fall was very pleasant with temperatures in the mid 60's and sunny days. Mornings like this were cool but nice, and with light sweaters they were very comfortable sitting outside at a table. Atiyah began with, "Where do we go from here David?"

"Good question! Guess it would be best if I move to San Francisco since I don't have a job and I don't have a home to go back to? I'd love to work for Doctors Without Borders but I don't know if that's possible now. Atiyah I am so angry with your brother I could kill him myself if he was still alive! It will take some time for me to lose this anger,I have to tell you."

Atiyah looked serious as she said, "Maybe you should have your own place first? I mean, I don't mind you moving in with me, since apts are so expensive in SF but you might want some space before getting too involved again in this relationship?"

"You know I want to be with you but I kinda think you're right. At this point how about I come back with you, stay awhile, and we make that decision at a later date. No promises, just take it a day at a time?"

"David, that's fine with me."

They walked along the Bosphorus in front of the old Dolmabahce Palace. It was a lot cooler here than it had been back in Baghdad but pleasant with a light sweater and the sun warming them. They spent most of the morning walking, talking, making plans and at times needing to just hold each other, thinking about all that had happened and how they had been brought together again. Atiyah stopped with anger in her voice, thinking of how she had been preyed upon by her brother. How hurt and angry she was to think he could do such a thing. She said to David,"I wonder how much his macho pride was involved in this attempt to kidnap me and use me in a suicide bombing so he could restore his honor! Damn his honor! Now he's dead! He was my family! I will forever be terrified of going to my homeland ever again! I am sure Allah would never condone such nonsense! I can say I am also glad I have turned away from any form of organized religion.

No God would require that we hate another human being or put ourselves above our neighbor who may not believe the same."

They were walking along the Bosphorus now and David stopped, turned to Atiyah, face red with rage, and cut the air with his fist, shouting, "God damn him! God damn him and all of them! They almost killed the one I love! The one I had given up hope on ever seeing again!! What sense does it make?" Atiyah moved in, hugged David for a long time. After some tears, lots of hugs, and a mutual "I love you," they moved on.

They visited the tourist areas which they had done on previous trips but still found exciting. Istanbul, formerly known as Constantinople and having endured being conquered by the Greeks, the Romans, the Turkomans, and Europeans and now by tourists who come from around the world to marvel at this ancient and huge metropolis which incorporates so many diverse cultures and ancient landmarks. From the Blue Mosque, the Istiklal District, the Grand Bazaar, the Topkapi Palace and so many more places this city draws the tourist back time and again.

This unique city which straddles two continents, Europe and Asia, two seas, the Sea of Marmara and the Black Sea and was for centuries the capital of the Roman Empire, the Byzantine Empire and the Ottoman Empire.

David had booked tickets for a flight back to San Francisco for the next day. Atiyah was feeling better but she still had nightmares the last couple of nights. She woke screaming and David had to hold her and share his similar experience which helped her know it was OK and would get better. She was excited and ready to bring this good man into her life.

EPILOGUE

The streets of Daly City were hilly and provided some great views of downtown San Francisco which was about 15 miles from Atiyah's apartment. Looking the other direction from the city they could see the bay and David always thought how different from Baghdad, which was flat and dusty and in the middle of a huge desert, though it also was built on the shores of the Tigris river. No blown up vehicles or blast holes in the road or walls! He still looked around for strangers or suspicious situations when he came out of their apartment, but more from habit than any real fear.

He was finished stretching and ready to start his run when he turned to see Atiyah come down the stairs in her running shorts. She looked so cute in yellow shorts striped with white, a matching yellow top and a scarf pulling her dark hair back. The scarf was for convenience not to hide her hair and face as in Baghdad. He went up to her and kissed her saying, "You are the prettiest girl in the world! Let's go!"

"You are right! Sweet Man! You know I can feel so at ease now! It's amazing and scary to me how millions of women in the world don't have this freedom. I love you and love, love, love this wonderful country!"

They ran about 5 miles and returned to their apartmentt, Atiyah's apartment if you wanted to be technical but more and more it was becoming their home. Atiyah showered and David made coffee for them . Atiyah came in to the kitchen and David said, "So you're on call this week end?"

"Yes, sorry."

"No, it's fine. I just I hope we can at least get downtown and go to the Wharf for lunch?"

"We'll see, I hope so too! David I have something to tell you. She gave him a flirty smile, "I was going to wait until lunch but I can't!"

David's mind flashed, *"Oh, oh! She's going to tell me she wants me to get my own place! Damn! Why didn't I see this coming?"*

Atiyah yelled out, "Surprise! You're going to be a daddy! I'm going to have a baby! I wanted to wait 'till I showed a little more but I just couldn't do it!" She came around his chair, hugging him tight. Letting the towel fall to the floor.! Are you happy!"

"Happy? "He jumped up from his chair, picking Atiyah up still hugging her tight and swinging her around.

"Happy!Happy! Happy!!" He put her down and knelt with his hand on her stomach, then kissed her tummy, "Mmmmmm. My baby! My baby!"

Atiyah was still wet but David didn't care.

Standing and kissing her he mumbled, "I'm delirious! I'm the happiest man in the world!"

"David I know we have been through so much and we've been caught between the hatred of Muslims, Jew, and Christians but we will raise our child to respect all religions and people and always keep world peace as our goal. Knowing you believe as I do in this simple wish makes me so very happy. Thank you David for being the man you are. I love you!"

WE INTERRUPT THIS WAR

We interrupt this war for doctors to heal, teachers to teach, and students to learn.

We interrupt this war to marvel at sunsets, listen to music, and to laugh.

We interrupt this war for poets to rhyme, sculptors to chisel, and writers to paint pictures with words.

We interrupt this war to plant tomatoes, mow the grass, and to smell the roses.

We interrupt this war to feed the hungry, build new schools, and to stamp out ignorance.

We interrupt this war to clean up the air, save the whales and to find a cure for cancer.

We interrupt this war to rebuild New Orleans, tickle babies and for world peace.

We interrupt this war for PTA meetings, band concerts, and high school graduations.

We interrupt this war for Girl Scout Cookies, church bake sales, and the Special Olympics.

We interrupt this war for Disneyland, the World Series, and the Super Bowl.

We interrupt this war for Halloween candy, Thanksgiving Turkey, and 4th of July fireworks.

We interrupt this war for Hanukkah, Christmas and Kwanza.

We interrupt this war to bring sons, daughters, sisters and brothers home.

And now we pause for a message from Our Sponsor: THOU SHALT NOT KILL.

Cappy Hall Rearick..